DORSET MAPS

SHIRE

Crokehorne

Barwick   Clyston   Lillington   Westhall
Etmynster   Bearehagard   Longburton
Suttonbingham   Clausworth   Pyme   Als Blake   The Vaile of Whithart
Lewcombe   Chedall   Lyghe   Holneste   Glansfeldendo
Charde   Wayford   Pen   N. Parret   Halstok   Chedall Stoke   Hermitage   Duntyshc
Whitstautou   Wynsham   Clapton   Seboro   Melburyosmond   Melbury bub   Hilsfeld
Mysterton   So. Parret   Mostern   E. Chelbury   Melburysaford   Vcombemetrevers   Mynterne mag. B.
Wambrok   Mostern   W. Chelbury   Euershot   Batcombe   Alto
PARTE OF   Cheddington   Coscombe   Frome quintan   Mynterne
Longbridge   Forde   Rowscham   Chantmene   Vpsidlinge   Vpcerne
Churchestocke   DEVON   Brodewindsor   Tollard welme   Wraxhall   So. Chahnington
Stockland   Memburj   Thorncombe   Bemyster   Penham   St. Nichol sidlinge   Biddle
Dalwood   SHIRE   Burstok   Lewson hull   pen   Hoke   Kencombe   Catstok   Nethere
Axmyster   Pittesdon   Abbot esstokes   Maperton   Chilfrome   Fors
ARTE   Hankchurch   Bettescombe   Pillesdon   N. Poreton   Madennewton   Godmauston
OF   Lambart cast   Hill   Crekelade   Netherbury   Mitton   Tollard mag.   Frampton   Grimston
Cullyton   Shute   Marshwood   Melplash   Porestoke   Tollardpua   Frome   Stratton
DEVON   Compine   pk.   Wotton   Whitchurch   Sunmesbore   Burpho   Nettlecombe   Eckerdon hill   Wauchurdy   Grimston
SHIRE   Musbure   Vplyme   Charmouth   Chidioh   Waldish   Longlother   Wenford   Southover   Mulcelford   Bradford peuill
Seton   Lyme   Stantongabriell   Byrton   Baunton   Askerswell   W. Compton   E. Compton   Longbridge   Stepelton   DORCHESTER
Beare   Axmouth   Shipton   Lytton   Litlebrudye   Blakdon Hill   olim DVRN   Martinstown
Punkcuall   Beksinton   Portesham   Frierwaddon   Muncton
MARE   Swire   Corton   Vpwey
Abotesburye   Reddon   B.
Buckland
Langton   W. Chek
BRITAN   NICVM   E. Cheker
E. Fete

MARE   BRITA   NICVM

1   5   10

William kip Sculp.

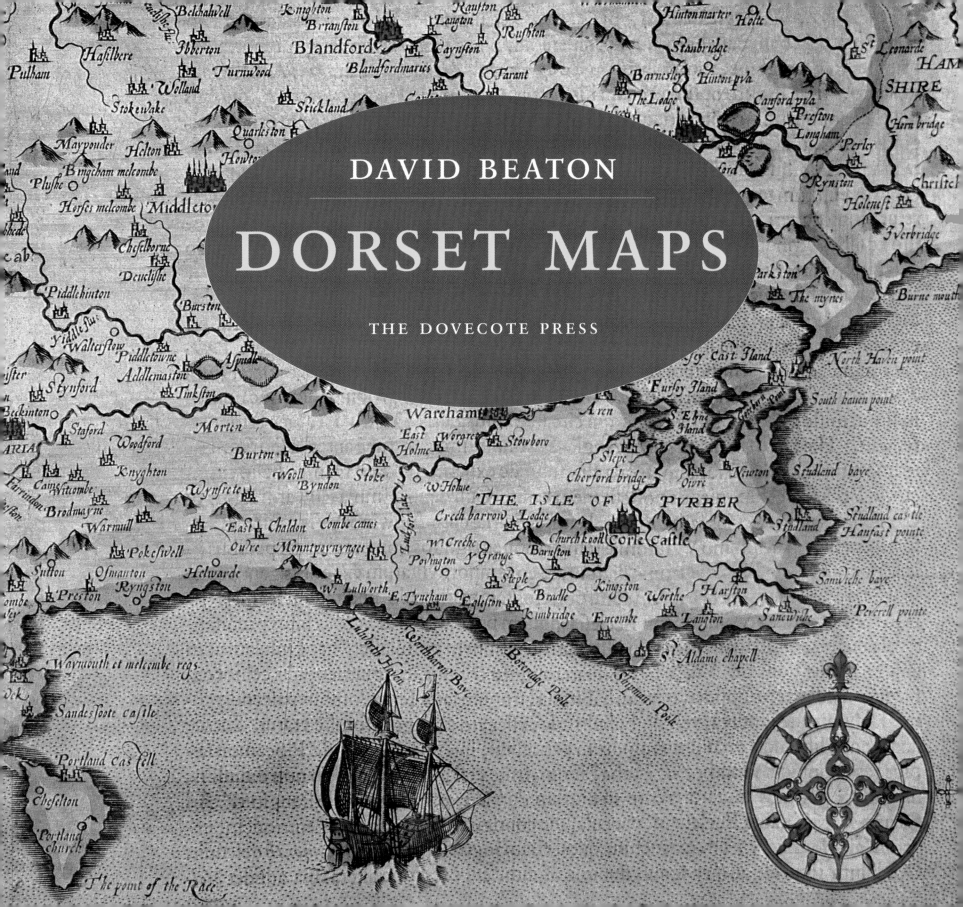

DAVID BEATON

DORSET MAPS

THE DOVECOTE PRESS

First published in 2001 by The Dovecote Press Ltd
Stanbridge, Wimborne, Dorset BH21 4JD

ISBN 1 874336 79 2

Designed by The Dovecote Press

Typeset in Monotype Sabon

Printed and bound by KHL Printing, Singapore

A CIP catalogue record for this book is available
from the British Library

1 3 5 7 9 8 6 4 2

Contents

Introduction

'Cartography is a sublime craft.'
FRA MAURO, CARTOGRAPHER TO THE COURT OF VENICE

You do not have to be a specialist to appreciate maps. As F.P. Sprent says in his introduction to Thomas Chubb's *Printed Maps*, 'the fascination of old maps is proverbial. As long as human nature remains unchanged so long will the unknown and the mysterious continue to possess an irresistible attraction for the majority of mankind.'

John Aubrey, the author of *Brief Lives*, wrote of Thomas Hobbes, the philosopher, that he 'tooke great delight to goe to the bookebinders' shops and lye gaping on mapps.' Perhaps Shakespeare has the last word on the subject in *Twelfth Night*. Maria, describing Malvolio to Sir Toby Belch, says: 'He does smile his face into more lines than are in the new map, with the augmentation of the Indies: you have not seen such a thing as 'tis; I can hardly forbear hurling things at him.'

Fortunately, most people faced with cartographic examples are not roused to such ire. In this clear reference to the age of discovery, it is evident that advances in map-making were sufficiently well known to make their way into everyday language. They were, indeed, exciting times. For the Tudors, it meant a new awareness of their place in the world and the need for outward expressions of self-esteem. This led to a blossoming of the Arts and Sciences and to an increase in travel. It was natural for people having a sense of belonging to a great nation to want a visible sign of nationhood; and what better way of recording their pride for future generations could there be than setting down on high quality hand-made paper an accurate topography of the whole country?

This is exactly what Christopher Saxton was commissioned to do by Thomas Seckford, a Master of the Requests to Queen Elizabeth I. Saxton set such a fine example, that British map-making was launched into a cartographic heritage unrivalled in the world. A significant part of this heritage is a long sequence of Dorset maps. These fascinating sheets of history chart the changing face of the county – the disappearance of forests, parks and woodland; the redefining of boundaries; the enclosure of land and changes in agriculture; the expanding network of roads; the effect of turnpikes; the impact of mail-coach and postal routes; the development of the railway system; the transformation of industry; and the corresponding waxing and waning of towns and villages.

This survey, dealing mainly with antique maps (more than 100 years old) from four successive centuries, looks at these changes and investigates the contribution made by cartographers, historians, publishers, engravers, surveyors, topographers, printers and booksellers, whose complex interrelationship led to the fine examples of cartography used as the illustrations in this book.

Each map has its own story to tell, both in terms of what information it can give us about the county and of its significance in the development of map-making. From the earliest, breathtakingly-striking Tudor view of coastal defences to the more mundane maps of the late nineteenth and early twentieth centuries, there has been a forward momentum, resulting in a unique and irreplaceable record for posterity.

The Sixteenth Century

BIRD'S-EYE VIEW OF
THE DORSET COAST, 1539

When is a map not a map? Should bird's-eye drawings of views, made before accurate surveying started, be included in a book about maps? I believe that they should, because they had the same function as a map: to give a coherent and reasonably accurate understanding of topography. Perhaps the leap of imagination required to move from the 'maplessness' of the period before 1550 to the explosion of maps thereafter – the leap from the bird's-eye view to the plan view – is not as strange as it seems. After all, the perspective view from an imagined, impossibly high hill or tower is not so far removed from the plan view, which is, conceptually, an image of the land as seen from directly above.

The earliest known perspective view of Dorset is a Tudor illustration measuring 1500 mm x 535 mm, viewed as if from inland, looking out to sea. It was drawn in the wake of a survey by Sir John Russell, one of the commissioners appointed by the Lord Chancellor, Thomas Cromwell, to 'search and defend the coasts' for Henry VIII at a time when war with France seemed imminent.

Sir John and his fellow commissioners, Sir Giles Strangeways and Sir John Horsey, surveyed the coast of Dorset in 1539 and their recommendations caused a grand defensive plan to be framed – which is what the illustration shows. Works were proposed at Bournemouth, Brownsea Island, Poole, Portland, Sandsfoot, the base of the Nothe at Weymouth and the end of the Cobb at Lyme Regis. The plan was never carried out in its

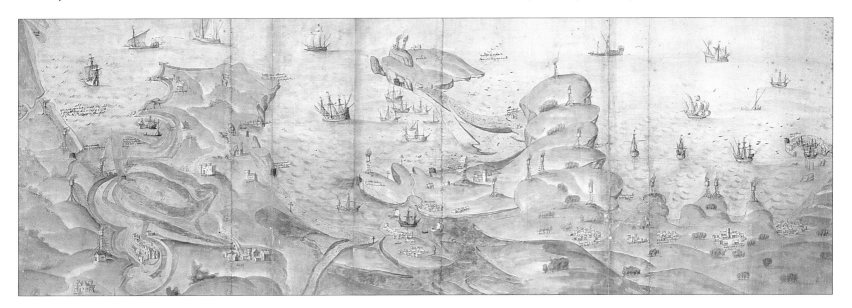

The Bird's-Eye View of the Dorset Coast, 1539

A detail from the Bird's-Eye View of 1539 showing the section from the mouth of the River Bourne (now Bournemouth) to just west of Portland Bill (top right). Melcombe Regis (Weymouth) is bottom right and Poole Harbour to the left. Note Corfe Castle and the deer on the Isle of Purbeck. The map is of particular importance to naval historians for its depiction of early Tudor boat design. This is the first of five maps of the Isle of Purbeck, which together provide a fascinating insight into the changing character of Purbeck: see also pages 13, 55, 59 and 69.

entirety; the Bournemouth, Poole and Lyme forts were dropped, and that at Brownsea was built by the burgesses of Poole, for there is no record of it among the list of royal forts.

As far as the fortifications around Weymouth and Portland are concerned, a defensive tower at Wyke Regis can be seen. Similarly Sandsfoot and Portland castles are clearly shown, and positioned to provide crossfire over the anchorage at Portland Road. Further east, the blockhouse at the foot of the Nothe at Weymouth can be distinguished. The view ranges from 'Chalke Roke' (the Needles) in the east (on the left) to 'The Cobbe of Lyme' in the west (on the right). The Cobb was first constructed in the thirteenth century with wooden piles and blocks of stone to provide shelter from the prevailing westerly winds. It has been periodically breached and rebuilt over the centuries, finally being reinforced in the nineteenth century with an exterior of more durable Portland stone. Poole Harbour is plainly well defended by the castle on Brownsea Island and the coast is liberally provided with fire-beacons. Two are shown on the downs above Weymouth and there is another on the Nothe. Two more beacons on Portland foreshadow the two lighthouses which were to be built two centuries later. A pleasant touch on a map produced for military purposes is the deer shown on the Isle of Purbeck.

An interesting sidelight is that the French ambassador was watching closely the progress of Henry's new defences and making frequent reports about them to his sovereign, Francis I. Those intended to protect Portsmouth and the Solent he went to see for himself, for he knew they were of vital strategic importance to the French government, but he did not come to Dorset, where the works were proceeding more slowly and were of less interest.

Dorset's potential contribution to Henry VIII's fledgling navy was substantial. Lyme, Bridport, Charmouth, Weymouth, Melcombe Regis and Poole all provided men and ships, the largest of which was the *Mary and John*, of 120 tons, belonging to Thomas Wade of Burton Bradstock.

CHRISTOPHER SAXTON, 1575

A map of Christopher Saxton's must be the jewel in the crown of any collection. Saxton was a surveyor and publisher, and though his dates remain uncertain we know that he flourished between 1570 and 1596. He was the first person to produce a printed set of county maps, and is deservedly regarded as the 'father of English map-making'. No one before him had produced an atlas consisting of detailed maps of sections of the country, and its magnificent scale set the standard for years to come. Each map was on a double page, with the exception of his native Yorkshire, whose great size required two joined sheets.

Saxton's map of Dorset, measuring 540 mm x 375 mm and printed in 1575 (four years before his *Atlas of the Counties of England and Wales* was published), is distinctive for a number of reasons. It has an extremely decorative cartouche, surrounded by ornamental strapwork and surmounted by the Royal Arms of Elizabeth, flanked by the Lion and the Dragon rampant. The Dragon was replaced by the Scottish Unicorn when James I became King. The other coat-of-arms is that of Thomas Seckford, Saxton's patron. Seckford was a Master of the Requests to Elizabeth I and without his support Saxton would never have been able to achieve all that he did.

Saxton's maps were finely engraved on copper plates by a team of English and Flemish engravers. There are two distinct lettering styles for place names. Larger towns and cities are in capital letters; script is used for the rest. The sea is dotted or 'stippled'. In the Dorset map a sea creature slips through the waves amongst sailing vessels and fishing boats. The fishing industry is also reflected in the hooked fish hanging from the underside of the cartouche. A large pair of dividers surmounts the scale. The hilly regions are depicted by a series of 'molehills' and the parks are bounded by railed fencing. No hundreds (administrative and legal districts dating from Saxon times) are detailed, although both roads and hundreds appear on the later issues of the atlas by Philip Lea.

Amongst much that is of interest on the map is its inclusion of the last of the ninety or so medieval deer parks, of which 17 still survived. All 6 containing deer in 1583 (Gillingham, Holt, Hooke, Melbury, Melcombe and Sherborne) are shown. The other parks included by Saxton are Marshwood, Crekelade, Blagdon, Athelhampton (spelt Addlemaston), Canford Parva and Canford Magna. Some forests are also shown: Gillingham Forest in the north of the county, Cranborne Chase in the north-east and Holt Forest in the east.

Gillingham, one of several deer parks in the county held directly by the crown, is an example of one which formed the core of a wider forest area, and from which deer were released to be hunted. Other parks were held by the Church or a succession of great nobles, such as the Earl of Gloucester

Christopher Saxton, 1575, 'father of English map-making'. Saxton's survey was the first to map the entire realm.

(Alderhill and Cranborne), the Earl of Pembroke (Alderholt), the Earl of Lincoln (Canford) and the Earl of March (Blagdon). Nearly all the parks passed through a variety of hands over the centuries. As local families, like the Martyns of Athelhampton and the Strangways of Melbury Sampford, grew in wealth and importance, each aspired to its own deer-park.

Idiosyncratic features are the piece of Devon tucked into the arm of the River Axe and the parish of Holwell being 'part of Somersetshire'. These anomalies continue to be shown until the redefining of county boundaries in the nineteenth century and local government reorganisation in the twentieth led to a more logical area of responsibility for the Dorset County Council (see

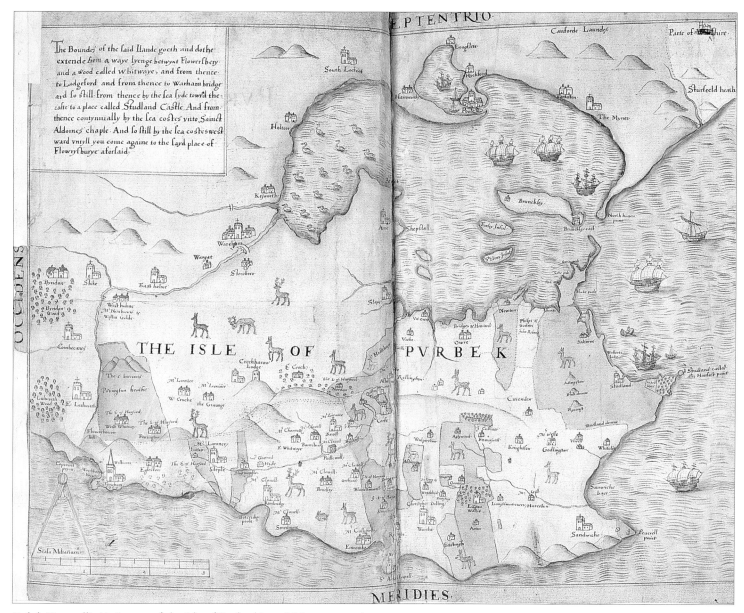

Ralph Treswell's 'A Survey of the Isle of Purbeck', 1586 (see page 15).

page 90). The most recent of these changes was the expansion of Dorset eastwards to include Bournemouth and Christchurch in 1974.

Another curiosity is the marking of a church at Newton on the Isle of Purbeck, since none was ever built. Nearby Ower was the principal port for the huge medieval trade in Purbeck limestone and marble. In the twelfth and thirteenth centuries thousands of fonts, tombstones and coffin-slabs of Purbeck marble, destined for cathedrals and churches all over England and in Europe, passed through Ower. Such was the volume of trade that in 1286 Edward I ordered the construction of a new town to the east of Ower, but there is no evidence that the planned market-place, harbour,

Portland and Weymouth, late sixteenth century, possibly by Robert Adams.

streets and building plots ever materialised. However, Newton rose to some prominence in the nineteenth century for a time, when clay was dug there and transported by tramway to the pier at the top of the Goathorn, the small promontory to the north.

There were many printings from Saxton's original plates by different publishers from the first edition of 1579 until those by Cluer Dicey in 1770. It is customary to give these editions a double-barrelled name, the first half being Saxton's, and the second half that of the publisher. The Saxton-Web, dated 1642, published in 1645 by William Web, has the Arms of Elizabeth replaced by those of Charles I and is sometimes known as the Civil War issue. The Saxton-Lea of Dorset was published by Philip Lea in 1689, containing town plans copied from John Speed. The Saxton-Willdey was published by George Willdey around 1731; the Saxton-Jefferys by Thomas Jefferys around 1749; and the Saxton-Dicey around 1770, a pale and worn final issue, from plates which were nearly two hundred years old. All of these re-issues are collectors' items, especially the Saxton-Web, regarded by some collectors as more of a rarity than the original.

RALPH TRESWELL, 1586

Estate maps range from little more than crude sketches to fully triangulated surveys showing the extent, value and ownership of land for taxation purposes. Accuracy was not crucial, as estate maps were intended to be read alongside their written 'awards'. Indeed, estate surveys carried out before the mid-sixteenth century were usually presented in written form, the maps, if any, being used merely as an illustration.

Estate maps started to appear in the 1570s and the early example shown is a Survey of the Isle of Purbeck by Ralph Treswell in 1586 (see page 13). As well as the general map, which measures 540 mm x 420 mm, there are detailed maps and descriptions of the manor of Studlande, the Manor or Lordshippe of Langton Wallis, Middlebury, Langton Farme, Newton Heath and Corfe Castle.

In the top left-hand corner there is a title cartouche containing Treswell's general description of Purbeck, written in well-spaced italic calligraphy: 'The Boundes of the said Ilande goeth and dothe extende from a waye lyenge betwyxt Flowersbery and a wood called Whitwaye, and from thence to Ludgeford and from thence to Warham bridge and so still from thence by the sea syde toward the easte to a place called Studland Castle. And from thence contynnially by the sea costes unto Sainct Aldomes chaple. And so still by the sea costes westward untyll you come againe to the sayd place of Flowrysburye aforesaid.'

In the north-east of Purbeck lies Studland, meaning 'grazing-land for horses', though by Treswell's day deer appear to be more common judging by the number dotted about on the map. Another ancient industry was the production of salt along the southern shores of Poole Harbour. There were 32 salterns or salt pans in the time of Domesday.

The mention of 'a place called Studland Castle' implies that the castle was no longer standing. However it may have been intact at the time of King John, who in 1205 landed at 'Stodlandt' whilst fitting out a fleet at Portsmouth for an expedition against France, and who returned there again a few years later.

At around the time of Treswell's map, another mapmaker, possibly Robert Adams, produced a coloured plan of the Isle of Portland, Melcombe and Weymouth, drawn on vellum, measuring 430 mm x 300 mm. In Weymouth Bay the inner beach is marked as 'The narrow' and the outer beach is called 'The shelf'. A 'Platforme' or landing-stage is depicted on the front at Melcombe. The entrance to the harbour is referred to as 'The haven'. 'The poynt' (Nothe Point) has a rocky outcrop off the headland named 'The Mixen', just as on today's Ordnance Survey Outdoor Leisure map. The Nothe itself is shown as having cultivated fields, the ploughed furrows being clearly visible.

'Sandfoot Castell' and 'Portland Castell' are prominent either side of 'Smalmouth Passage'. On Portland itself 'Churchhope' and 'Cheseltowne' are the only places of habitation marked. On the mainland the place names are easily recognisable. To the east the distinctive Dorset coastline is pictured in relief as far as Ringstead Bay. Careful study of the sea in Weymouth Bay reveals a faintly drawn compass, bearing the traditional words of orientation: Septentrio for north, Meridies for south, Oriens for east and Occidens for west.

Engraved by William Kip in *Camden's Britannia*, 1607. Editions of *Camden's Britannia* spanned an astonishing 256 years.

The Seventeenth Century

WILLIAM CAMDEN, 1607

William Camden (1551-1623) was a contemporary of Christopher Saxton and was educated at St Paul's School and Magdalen College, Oxford. He became headmaster of Westminster School and many of his writings were undertaken in the school holidays.

Although not a map-maker, he had a profound influence on the course of map-making, because he provided the vehicle for some of the finest maps ever produced. These appeared over a number of years in his scholarly history of Britain from pre-Roman times, *Britannia*. The numerous editions of *Britannia* spanned an astounding 256 years, and the list of publishers, printers and engravers reads like a roll of honour of cartography.

Commonly referred to as *Camden's Britannia*, it was first published in 1586, in Latin, with no maps. It was not until the sixth edition, in 1607, that a cartographical breakthrough occurred, because this edition, published by George Bishop, was the first work to contain a set of county maps of England and Wales, with each county engraved on a separate sheet. The 1607 edition had Latin text on the back of the maps, whereas the two later editions had plain backs. The 1610 edition was also published by Bishop, and Andrew Hebb published the 1637 edition, in which plate numbers were added to many of the maps.

The Dorset map in this earliest Camden series, 385 mm x 275 mm, was engraved by William Kip and looks like a scaled-down Saxton, which is exactly what it is. Indeed, some of the other county maps from the series retain Saxton's name under the scale and have sometimes been mistaken for an original Saxton. This example is from the Latin-backed 1607 edition. It is typical of the very earliest style of cartography, in which features such as hills and rivers are drawn on a much exaggerated scale. The maps are very accurate for their period. It has been shown that if all the county maps were to be pieced together in the style of a jig-saw, the result would be a good approximation to the actual shape of England and Wales.

Although the similarities between Saxton's 1575 map and Camden's version are much as one would expect of maps that were copied one from the other, there are differences. The more southerly of the two Holt Forest parks has disappeared on Camden's map, but an extra one has appeared near Affpuddle.

Camden gives greater prominence than Saxton to the ecclesiastical centres with his large, many-spired red symbols. Milton Abbas is written as Middleton, the original name of the town, from which Abbot William Middleton probably took his own name. Abbot Middleton was responsible for the building of the fine vaulting of the north and south transepts of Milton Abbey in the late fifteenth century. The only remaining monastic building (apart from the Abbey Church) is the Abbot's Hall, currently the Milton Abbey school dining-hall, which was also his work.

Maps from the earliest series of Camden are termed either Saxton-Kip or Saxton-Hole, the Kip and Hole referring not to the publishers, but to the engravers, William Kip and William Hole. Dozens of other editions of *Camden's Britannia* appeared over more than two centuries, until the last one published by Samuel Tymms in 1842, entitled *Camden's Britannia Epitomised and Completed*. Most of the editions of this long-running work contained maps, many by distinguished engravers.

JOHN SPEED, 1610

The name of John Speed (1552-1629) is probably the best known of all British map-makers, and copies of his maps are in great demand, especially early editions. He was responsible for two new features of map-making: inset plans of county or principal towns, and the delineation of parish hundreds with dotted lines.

In the eleventh century territorial divisions called hundreds formed the basis of the organisation of public justice and the administration of public finance throughout southern England. Unlike the hundreds of the Midlands, which were remodelled into roughly symmetrical regions during the tenth century, the ones in Wessex were never regularised by an act of state and they remained of an irregular size, many of them tiny compared to their neighbours. These administrative and legal districts continued to be the basis of political organisation for the next eight centuries.

Speed himself surveyed the majority of the new town plans, hence the wording 'Scale of Pases' under the dividers. This was a time-honoured scale based on a natural walking pace, which can be remarkably uniform, using the legs of a skilled surveyor like Speed. On visiting Dorset, he was struck by the quality of the air, which he described as 'good and of an healthful constitution.' He was equally impressed by the fertility of the county.

The Dorset map, measuring 510 mm x 380 mm, abandons the custom of indicating compass points with Latin – Oriens (rising sun), Occidens (setting sun), Meridies (midday sun) and Septentrio (the seven stars of the Great Bear) – in favour of anglicised East, West, South and North. Engraved by Dutchman Jodicus Hondius, the map is entitled: 'Dorsetshyre, with the Shyre-towne Dorchester described, as also the Armes of such noble families as have bene honoured with the Titles thereof since the Normans Conquest to this present anno 1610.'

The coats-of-arms are ranged decoratively in the lower left-hand corner. The first represents Osmund, Earl of Seez in Normandy, who was made Bishop of Salisbury, Lord Chancellor and Earl of Dorset by William the Conqueror. He died in 1099 and his shield is blank, because there was no formal system of heraldry until a sudden flowering of the art between 1135 and 1155.

The second coat-of-arms is that of John de Beaufort, son of John of Gaunt, Earl of Somerset. He was created Marquis of Dorset by Richard II, as was the owner of the third coat-of-arms, Thomas Grey, by Edward IV. The fourth belongs to Thomas Sackville Esq, who was born in 1536, was created 1st Earl of Dorset by James I and died in 1608. He is accorded especial honour on Speed's map, because his escutcheon appears again on a plinth to the right of the town plan.

Other decorative features are the royal coat-of-arms, the sea monsters, the galleons in full sail, the swag-holding maidens atop the armorial cartouche and the horn-blowing merman beside 'The Scale of English Miles'.

The inset plan of Dorchester was the first map of the town to be printed. The livestock pound and church in Fordington, on the right, are prominent and there are large areas of open farmland inside the remains of the Roman wall (designated 'The ruins of the ould wall' on the left-hand side of the plan). The street pattern is largely accurate, although Trinity Street is missing and many of the angles are wrong. We know that High West Street was fully lined with houses, whereas Speed shows some gaps. However, he makes allowance for the growth of the town, with back streets developing.

The parks and boundaries of the hundreds are well defined with colour wash. The hundreds were a curious combination of political, geographical and social convenience, so-called because they were originally supposed to contain 100 hides. A hide (roughly 120 acres, but varying in size according to the quality of the land) was an area of arable plus waste land that was reckoned to be the amount needed to support a substantial free family with its dependents.

Many boundaries followed natural features, such as rivers, hills and coasts. The same boundary anomalies found on the Saxton map occur, such as the part of Devon on the Dorset side of the River Axe and the detached part of Somerset in Holwell.

The maps in Speed's atlas were originally intended to illustrate his *History of Great Britain*. The text on the back of each map is a description of the county, based on Camden's earlier researches. It is likely that the plates for the maps were engraved

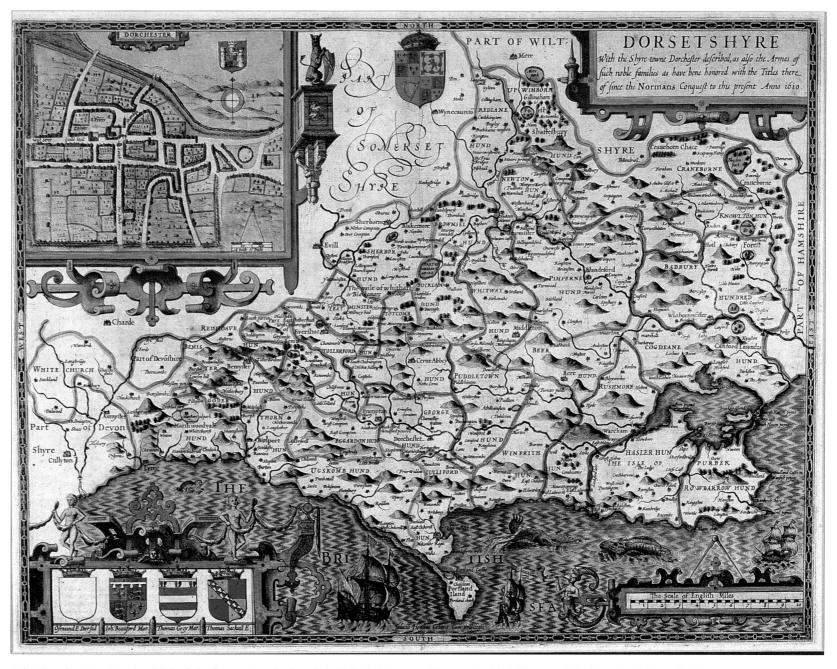

John Speed, 1610. Speed published the first national atlas of the British Isles, grandiloquently titled *Theatre of the Empire of Great Britaine.*

in Amsterdam. Hondius, the Dutch engraver mentioned earlier, was given the contract for the work, but he spent some time working in London, where he married the sister of Pieter Van den Keere (see page 23), before returning to Amsterdam, to take over Mercator's business in 1604, so it is possible that the first edition was printed in London.

There is no doubt that credit for the first national atlas of the British Isles lies firmly at the door of John Speed, in the form of his monumental *Theatre of the Empire of Great Britaine*, published in 1611, containing 67 folio maps under the grandiloquent sub-title of 'Presenting an Exact Geographie of the Kingdomes of England, Scotland, Ireland and the Iles adioyning: With the Shires, Hundreds, Cities and Shire-townes, within ye Kingdome of England, divided and described by John Speed.'

This lavishly illustrated book, which ran to some 15 subsequent editions over the next 160 years, has graced many a library in great stately homes. Estimates of the total number printed are as high as three thousand, which was only possible by re-touching important details. Some of the later impressions are very weak, which is why early editions are preferred.

In 1631, not long after his death, a portrait was published of John Speed, engraved by Salomon Savery. Commenting on the portrait, the Reverend Mr. Granger records that 'he died on 28th July, 1629, having had twelve sons and six daughters by one wife,' – a fitting epitaph for this prolific map-maker.

MICHAEL DRAYTON, 1612

This must be the most unusual of all maps of Dorset. This is partly because it was not intended as a correct geographical representation, but more as a decorative accompaniment to the author's poems in his *Poly-Olbion* or *Chorographical description of Tracts, Rivers, Mountains, Forests and other Parts of this renowned Isle of Great Britain*. Measuring 330 mm x 250 mm, it does not have the usual title, plate number or scale, but some may consider that we are amply compensated by the nude female bathers adorning the rivers and the huntresses armed for the chase in the forests. Cherubs pour water from pitchers to create the sources of rivers and the sea is depicted by a series of silky ripples.

Drayton's second song in *Poly-Olbion* begins:

'THRO' the Dorsetian fields that lie in open view,

My progress I againe must seriouslie pursue,

From Marshwood's fruitfull vale my journey on to make . . .'

and he discourses in high-flown language, but with accurate local knowledge, on many Dorset names:

'Bert-Port [Bridport] which hath gain'd

That praise from every place, and worthilie obtain'd,

Our cordage from her store, and cables should be made,'

a reference to an Act of Parliament of Henry VIII, enacting that hemp 'growing within five miles of the town shall be sold there and in no other place, and that no person but the inhabitants shall manufacture ropes and netting', in order to maintain the quality of the product, upon which the Royal Navy depended for all its tackling.

The description of Portland is especially interesting:

'Her rugged front empal'd on every part with rocks,

Though indigent of wood, yet fraught with woolly flocks:

Most famous for her folke, excelling with the sling

Of anie other heere this land inhabiting.'

Generations of quarrymen, coupled with Portland's relative isolation, produced a breed of tough and independent people who convinced themselves (and Hardy, amongst others) that they were a different race in appearance, habits and customs from those on the mainland. On the map that accompanies his novels Hardy calls Portland the 'Isle of Slingers'.

In an interesting reference to the Blackmore Vale, the poet wishes

'Thou never by that name of White Hart hadst been known,

But stiled Blackmore still, which rightly was thine own . . .',

an allusion to the legend of White Hart Silver, annually and in perpuity paid into the Royal Exchequer by Sir John de la Lynde, and subsequent owners of his land, as a punishment for hunting down and killing a beautiful white hart, whose life had been spared in an earlier chase by Henry III. The legend has it that de la Lynde and his hunting companions were imprisoned and fined heavily, in addition to the penance described above. The place of the stag's death was reputed to be at a bridge in Pulham, thenceforth known as King-stag Bridge, the name by which it is still known. For more than five centuries the name Vale of Whitehart was adopted, appearing on maps from Christopher Saxton onwards until it began to be dropped by map-makers in the late eighteenth century.

Turning from Drayton's writings to his curious cartography, it is noticeable that the goddess on 'The Ile of Wyght' is much

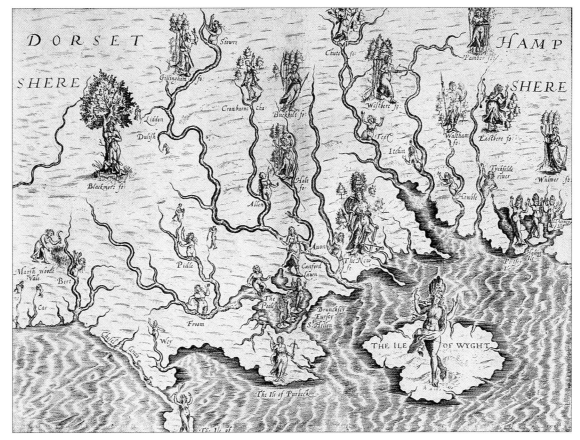

Michael Drayton, 1612. The map was drawn to accompany a collection of Drayton's poems, *Poly-Olbion*.

larger than any of the other maidens and is wearing a spectacular plumed headdress. The engraver, William Hole, gives her a 'classical foot', a trait where the second toe protrudes beyond the big toe, which was regarded in Elizabethan times as endowing the owner with a special physical attraction. The fingers of her left hand are also strangely elongated.

As is apparent from the map, Drayton's poetical musings were largely inspired by the rivers, which are personified in *Poly-Olbion*. In a reference to the destruction of Blackmore Forest,

'Whose big and lordlie oakes once bore as brave a sale,

As they themselves that thought the largest shades to spred,'
Froome bewails 'her mother Blackmore's state.' Running to comfort her,

'While Froome was troubl'd thus . . .,

The Piddle . . . bestir'd her nimble feet,

In falling to the Poole her sister Froome to meet.'

When it was first published in 1612, *Poly-Olbion* contained eighteen maps. A subsequent edition was published in 1613, where numbers were added. The last edition appeared in 1622, with ten extra maps and twelve additional verses. The numbers on the maps are not plate numbers, but refer to the page number of the text.

Nobody knows how many copies of the three editions were printed, but the work did not enjoy great popularity in its day and a map from any edition is regarded as a rarity.

Michael Drayton died in 1631, at the age of 68, and was buried in Westminster Cathedral, where a statue was erected by the Countess of Dorset to the memory of 'this modest and amiable man.'

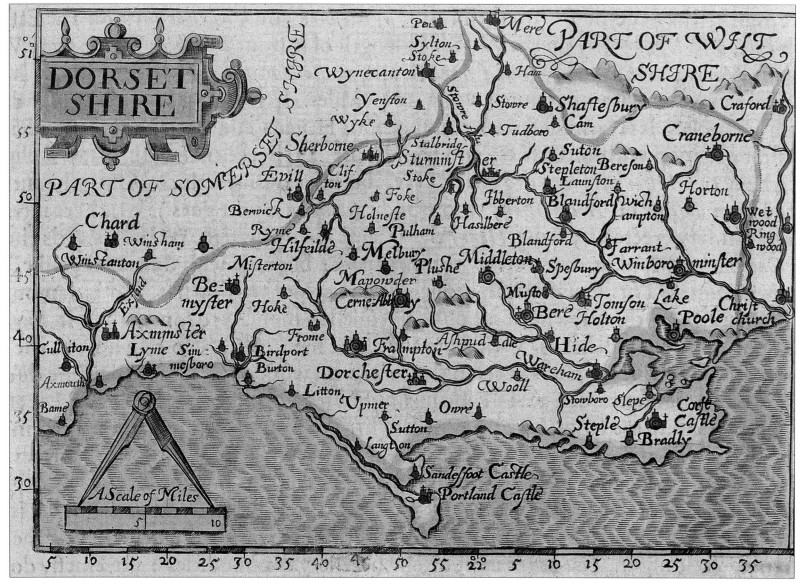

John Bill, 1626. This rare miniature map was the first of Dorset to carry a reference to latitude and longitude.

JOHN BILL, 1626

This beautiful map, measuring 120 mm x 80 mm, comes from *The Abridgement of Camden's Britannia*, published by John Bill in 1626. At first sight, the maps from this little atlas can be mistaken for Pieter Van den Keere's 'miniature Speeds'. However, the maps were the first from a British county series to carry a reference to latitude and longitude, in the left-hand and lower margins, and it is this that gives them their unique stamp.

Based on the maps of Camden, they bear the unmistakable imprint of Saxton: the three-dimensional strapwork round the cartouche, the familiar dividers over the scale of miles, the 'molehills' for higher ground and the 'forked lightning' river systems. This example has original colouring, confirmed by the telltale seepage through to the other side of the paper.

Half a century must pass before a county map showing roads is printed. There are many fewer place names than on Van den Keere's map, but this gives it a less cluttered aspect. Wyke Regis is omitted, and as in the 'miniature Speed', neither Melcombe Regis nor Weymouth is shown. Significantly in view of their importance as defensive positions, Sandsfoot and Portland Castles stand out even more prominently than on Van den Keere's, because they are the only names engraved on the sea.

The 1626 edition of Bill's *Abridgement* was the only one to be issued and is unlikely to have run to more than a few hundred copies. In common with other miniature atlases, it met with a high mortality rate.

Regarded by many collectors as the most rare of all the county atlases, *The Abridgement* is an exciting find when one comes to light. Individual maps are also extremely scarce.

PIETER VAN DEN KEERE, 1627

This immensely skilled and prolific Dutch engraver's early work included a set of miniature map plates based mainly on Saxton's. He engraved these from 1599 onwards, including maps of Scotland and Ireland. Had he decided to publish them in atlas form he would have been the first person to complete an atlas of the British Isles – an honour that fell to John Speed.

A later publisher, George Humble, reissued Speed's atlas in 1627, 1632 and 1646. To coincide with each of these editions, he reprinted Van den Keere's plates, also in atlas form, referring to them as 'miniature Speeds' and using Speed's popularity to encourage their sales. He re-worked the plates (acquired from Joan Blaeu, who had first published them in atlas form in 1617), converting the Latin county titles into English. He also printed

Pieter Van den Keere, 1627.

an English text on the back and gave each map a plate number in the lower right hand corner, number 8 in the case of Dorset. The map is liberally dotted with towns and villages and is a masterpiece of cartography in miniature.

The Dorset map measures 120 mm x 85 mm, and the text in the atlas relating to Dorset refers to the 'many sweet and fresh running springs', forming rivers at whose mouths are harbours, 'whereby Vessels of burden discharge their rich Treasures,' and the sea which 'with open hand distributeth her gifts all along the South of this Shore'.

The 'rich Treasures' were chiefly cargoes of textiles; there was a healthy trade in woollen cloth, not merely from Dorset but, via Dorset ports, from elsewhere in England, with ports such as Rotterdam and Morlaix. Linen cloths like 'duck' for sailors' uniforms, and the coarse linen still known as 'Holland' until the last century, were imported via Rotterdam, and 'lockram', linen used in furnishing and decorating, from Morlaix (see also Joan Blaeu, page 25, and Dodsley and Cowley, page 44).

Humble's text continues: 'Commodities arising in the Countie are chiefly Wools and Woods in her North, where the Forrests are stored with the one, and the pleasant greene Hilles with the other. The inner part is overspread both with Corne and Grasse, and the Sea yieldeth the *Inulis Plocamos* [samphire, whose Linnaean name today is *inula*], a Shrub growing not unlike the Coral without any leafe; besides her other gifts, turning all to great gaine which the more is made manifest by the many Market-Townes in this Shire, whereof Dorcester is the chiefe.'

If framed, examples of miniature Speeds can be double-glazed, showing the text on the reverse, as in the case of this uncoloured 1627 copy, which reveals a small section of watermark, as well as the distinctive wire-lines always found in handmade paper. It is an exceptionally clear example. Every detail is firm and dark, every dot of stippling on the strapwork around the cartouche is plain to the eye and every zigzagging ocean wave helps to highlight the well-defined coastline. Conversely, examples from the 1646 edition can be less clear, because by this time some of the plates were showing signs of wear. Nonetheless, examples from any edition are well worth having in a collection.

JACOB VAN LANGEREN, 1635

This rare map, just 100 mm square (including its distance table), was engraved by Jacob Van Langeren for Matthew Simons' atlas *A Direction for the English Traviller* in 1635. After Simons' death Thomas Jenner acquired the plates and published his own set of maps in 1643, under the same title.

Distance tables were the invention of the cartographer, John Norden, who introduced them in 1625, in his *intended guyde for English travailers*. For the first time distances between towns were detailed, in addition to the marking of roads, which was another of Norden's innovations. Even so, map-makers continued to issue maps without showing roads for the next century or so. The distance tables were an important innovation, and such is their value that modern road atlases still include them today.

The place names on the distance table are an indication of their relative importance at the time the map was made. Marshwood, now a tiny hamlet, was at one time a medieval 'honour' (a group of manors held by one lord). It was the seat of Baron Galfridus de Mandeville and was the only honour in the entire county. There were two large richly-wooded adjoining parks, Marshwood and Crekelade. Now the parks are gone and all that remains of de Mandeville's castle are some stone walls and a wide ditch, nearly filled up, which is the remains of the moat, originally enclosing an area of about two acres. Here the foundations of the castle's chapel, St. Mary's, were discovered in 1839. Along the northern edge of the parks ran a medieval road, which traversed the Marshwood Vale from south-east to north-west and is still largely in use today, albeit a country lane.

The map illustrated, brightly highlighted by a contemporary colourist, appeared some fourteen years later in the next edition of 1657. There is a telltale difference between this map and the one in the edition of 1643. Along the dogtooth edge of the table there are numbers, where the rows and columns of like towns meet, showing the distance of that town from London. In earlier editions, these are absent.

Though the scale of these maps is so small, the adjoining counties contain the names of 'some confining townes', a further means of assisting the traveller in his quest for relevant

Thomas Jenner's 1657 distance table has an extra row of mileages, showing the distance from London.

information. The small wedge-shaped space above the county contains a surprisingly comprehensive distribution of towns and cities. Bath, Wells and Salisbury are all included and the map reaches as far north as Malmesbury, a leading source of the wool on which so much of Dorset's prosperity depended.

The text in the atlas referring to Dorset begins with the numbered hundreds of the county, followed by an alphabetical list of all the towns and villages, with the hundred to which it belongs beside each one (some of which are below the map itself, continuing on the reverse).

After Thomas Jenner's death in 1673, the plates were passed to John Garrett, who published a further edition of the work in 1677, and a final one in about 1680. Thus those innovative travellers' maps had a good run for their money, spanning over half the century.

JOAN BLAEU, 1645, AND JAN JANSSON, 1646

In 1645 Joan Blaeu published a county atlas of England and Wales. It was part of his *Atlas Novus* and was based mainly on the researches of Saxton and Speed. In this work, Blaeu set standards of style and calligraphy that have never since been surpassed. Ornamental cartouches surrounded the names of the counties, superbly presented armorials lined the insides of the borders and in many cases the maps in the atlases were hand-coloured before they were issued, sometimes highlighted in gold.

The map illustrated, measuring 500 mm x 380 mm, with Latin text on the back, has a brightly coloured red and gold cartouche flanked by bales of wool and hemp. These represent the two main cash crops of the county at that time, sheep on the downlands for wool and hemp for the manufacture of ropes and netting.

Wool had been England's greatest trading currency since medieval times, a commodity highly valued throughout Europe and the Mediterranean. Dorchester produced broadcloth and serge, Sherborne, woollen cloth, whilst Lyme Regis produced lace and undertook some cloth-finishing, although at the time when this map was produced, Lyme, hitherto one of the leading textile ports, was still recovering from the siege of the previous year, when the town had staunchly held out for Parliament against Royalist troops under Prince Maurice.

In 1622 button-making was introduced to Shaftesbury by Abraham Case, a retired soldier, who had studied the traditional craft in Belgium and France while on military service. He built up a successful family business, based on out-workers from the surrounding villages, who produced the buttons in their own homes and brought them to the depot in the town. Shaftesbury became the centre of manufacture for the traditional Dorset buttons, which were based on a disc of sheep's horn covered in linen and then worked with thread made from wool or silk.

The buttons were used throughout England and must have been regarded as the height of fashion, for just four years after Blaeu's atlas was published, in 1649, the silk waistcoat worn by King Charles I on the day of his execution bore 'High Top' buttons of Case's own manufacture. Case outlived his monarch

Joan Blaeu, 1645. Son of Willem Blaeu, globe and instrument maker, Joan Blaeu beat his father's rival Jan Jansson in the race to produce a new atlas of the British Isles, *Atlas Novus*. One of the most finely engraved maps of Dorset ever produced, the decoration is colourful and eye-catching. The Blaeu family business came to an abrupt end when its Amsterdam premises were destroyed by fire in 1672.

by some nine years, dying in 1658. Eventually over thirty varieties of Dorset button were produced, ranging from the tall 'High Top' to the tiny buttons, known as 'Mites', designed for baby clothes. Tragically, the trade died almost overnight in the middle of the nineteenth century, when button-making machines were introduced, producing buttons at such low cost that the hand-made variety were priced out of the market, causing great hardship and forcing many to emigrate.

As for the manufacture of ropes and netting, Bridport's importance grew from the thirteenth century with the demand for naval and mercantile cordage, and it has remained the centre for rope-making in Britain. Many types were produced, and those sentenced to the gallows were said to have been 'stabbed with a Bridport dagger'. The importance of the town was underlined by its allocation of two parliamentary seats for nearly six centuries. Bridport's harbour, West Bay, now silting up, was formerly a shipbuilding centre of some importance. It contributed 19 small ships to the Fleet in the Napoleonic wars, all rigged with Bridport rope.

On this map, as on many others of Dutch origin, an interesting detail about the colouring of the coats-of-arms is revealed. There were two simple codes for colouring. Either there was a guiding letter, e.g. 'G' for Gules (red), or 'B' for Bleu (blue), or there was a system of engraving the background of the shield (e.g. vertical lines for red, or horizontal lines for blue). Unfortunately, the Dutch exchanged the lines for red and blue, the two most important colours in heraldry. This would not have mattered if all Dutch maps had been coloured in the Netherlands, but many were coloured elsewhere. So, where the bars on the arms of Thomas Grey, Marquis of Dorset, are coloured blue (correctly) on the Speed map, they are coloured red (incorrectly) on the Blaeu map.

They are likewise incorrectly coloured on copies of two other Dutch maps of Dorset, one published by Jan Jansson in 1646 (measuring 495 mm x 380 mm), and illustrated here in black and white; the other by Schenk and Valk in 1680, which was a re-working of the Jansson plate and is almost identical in size.

Jan Jansson, an eminent cartographer, printer and publisher, was a contemporary and leading rival of Joan Blaeu's father, Willem Blaeu, globe and instrument maker, who founded the

Jan Jansson, 1646.

Blaeu family business in 1599. Jansson was determined to be the first to produce an atlas of the British Isles, but he was beaten to it by the Blaeus. A French edition of Jansson's atlas (also entitled *Atlas Novus*) was issued in 1646, just one year after Joan Blacu's *Atlas Novus*. French, Dutch and German editions of Jansson's atlas followed during the next decade, with a final Latin edition in 1659.

The Blaeus' output of atlases, on the other hand, was prodigious over a period of nearly thirty years. Editions in French, Latin, German and Dutch followed the 1645 Latin and French editions, and there was even one incomplete (and rare) last edition in Spanish, dated 1672, a disastrous year for the Blaeus, because their premises in Amsterdam caught fire and much of the plant, including irreplaceable copper plates, was destroyed.

RICHARD BLOME, 1671

It has been said of Richard Blome that he left his mark in the map world more as a plagiarist than as a true contributor to British cartography. In 1696, Bishop William Nicholson described Blome's *Britannia*, published in 1673, as 'a most entire piece of theft out of Camden and Speed'. We know that his smaller atlas, entitled *Speed's Maps Epitomised* and published eight years later in 1681, was engraved at the same time as his *Britannia* and by the same engravers. Although the maps in the smaller atlas were crude reductions of Speed's original work, it appears to have had more success than the *Britannia*. It was published in three editions; the last, in 1693, involving the publication of the maps in a new edition called *Cosmography and Geography*.

The map illustrated, measuring 250mm x 190mm, from *Britannia*, is on paper with a large watermark depicting a jester and is dated 1671. If you compare this map with Blaeu's, published 26 years earlier, the sequence of five parks down the eastern edge of the county is still very noticeable. They are, from north to south, Blagdon, Woodlands, Holt, Canford Great Park and Canford Little Park. In the south-west, Crekelade and Marshwood can still be seen, but Crekelade, always the lesser park of the two, is no longer shown with any park-pales. In the west the royal forest of Blackmoor is still well defined, but in the north Gillingham Park is no longer marked, the word Forest simply being written in its place. The decline of Gillingham Forest dates from 1624, when its enclosure was commissioned by James I, which led to riots of local people objecting to the loss of their common rights, between 1626 and 1630. This once great forest contained King's Court near Gillingham, the most frequented of King John's twenty Dorset hunting lodges after Corfe. As royal finances dwindled and government became centralised in London, the royal houses fell from twenty in 1272 to six in 1485, foreshadowing the eventual decline of the forest itself. King's Court, once a thriving community with a chapel and plentiful accommodation, is now no more than rectangular earthworks on the outskirts of Gillingham.

Undeniably, Blome's engraving lacks the fine quality of the Speed original, but on the other hand, it could be argued that Blome filled an important gap, considering that the many publications in the market at the time were reprints or reissues of John Speed's maps. In this instance, the purchaser could buy a version of a well-established map with the additional 'Table of the Divitions and Hundreds in DORSETSHIRE'. This is the first time that a list of hundreds appears on a map of Dorset, and although the engraving of the letters for the divisions and the numbers for the hundreds is incredibly roughly executed, they show up clearly amongst the names of the towns and villages. As a ready reference, this is an extremely useful map, not too large, with important political information, fulfilling a need not supplied by Speed's maps.

Blome was also one of the earliest to finance his maps by subscription, so whether we admire his maps or not, we have to give him credit for his shrewd business sense. Some collectors find in Blome's maps a spontaneity of execution which appeals to them, which is particularly true of maps from the first edition of 1673, such as this one. It has already been pointed out that the engraving is crudely executed, yet it has a flamboyance of incision that gives it an unusually fresh appearance. The three boats are almost impressionistic in style. The cartouche in the left-hand corner has some fantastic fish with spiny fins and gaping mouths, surmounted by the armorial of Humphrey Weld. The S-shapes on either side of the cartouche look as if the engraver did not have time to finish decorating them properly, before the plate went off to the publisher. Or did he want to leave the right-hand S-shape free of cross-hatching, so as not to draw the eye away from the main subject, the map?

The wording in the cartouche is as follows: 'A General Mapp of Dorsetshire, With its Divitions, and Hundreds, described by Ric. Blome by his Majestys Especiall command, To ye Honourable Humphrey Weld of Lulwoth Castle Esq, Governour of his Majestys Isle & Castles of Portland and Sandesfoot &c:, This Mapp is humbly dedicated by Rich Blome.'

Like Speed Blome adopts the use of the points of the compass on the borders instead of the Latin Oriens, Occidens, Meridies and Septentrio favoured by Blaeu, Van den Keere and other mapmakers of the seventeenth century or earlier.

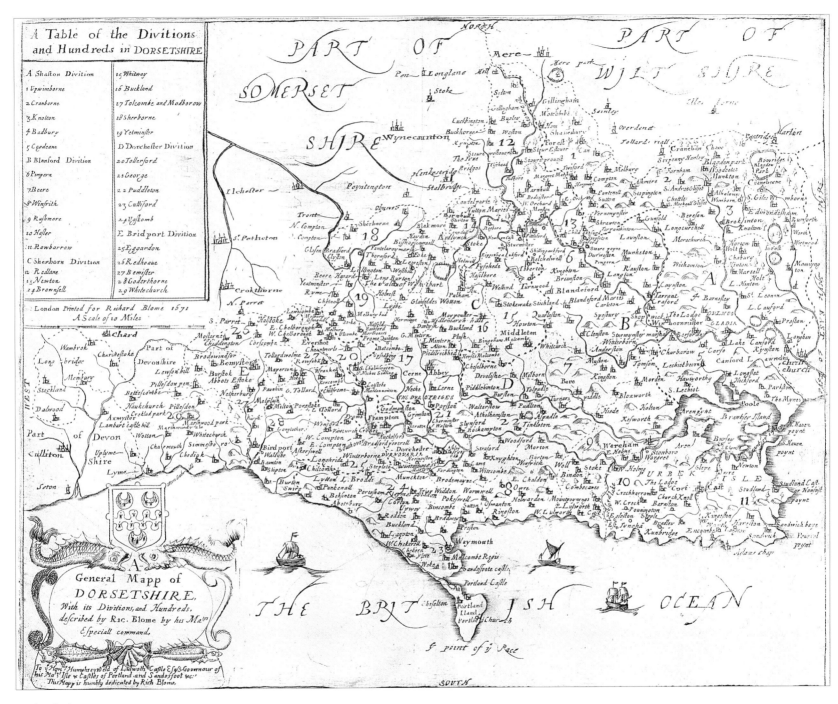

Richard Blome, 1671.

JOHN OGILBY, 1675

John Ogilby is regarded by many collectors as the most important name in cartography since Christopher Saxton, because the hundred strip roads that *Britannia* contained, depicting detailed routes through England and Wales, were a completely new concept. For the first time a single road could be followed, from departure point to destination, by means of a continuously scrolling ribbon, on a scale large enough to show not only not only the usual rivers, hills and county boundaries, but also bridges, crossroads and local landmarks.

The traveller was now provided with points of reference at sufficiently frequent intervals not only to reassure him about his direction (each strip carries a directional compass rose), but to remind him of the distances involved. A ready calculator of distances from London is marked in miles and furlongs the length of the route; it was only a matter of simple arithmetic to calculate the distance from one town to the next, and thus the likely travelling time.

The map in this example, from the 1675 first edition, follows the course of the Great Western Post Road (or West Road, now the A30), still one of the major arterial routes to the West Country. The title describes the route as:

> 'The Continuation of the Road from
> LONDON to the LANDS END
> Commencing at Andover in Hants &
> Extending to Crookhorn [Crewkerne] com. Somerset
> Containing 67 miles 6 furlongs viz:
> To SALISBURY 18 miles to Shaftesbury 19 miles 4 furl:
> To SHERBORN 15 miles 4 furl: & to Crookhorn 14 mi: 6 furl:'

The embellishments surrounding the title give an insight into the everyday costume of the period. The two men and their dog have been out shooting and the woman, in her wide country hat, is showing her basket of produce to her child.

After its first appearance at Andover at the base of strip F – G, the road continues through Winchester and Salisbury before rising onto the ridgeway. The usual route for an ancient trackway was along the crest of a ridge, with roads branching off to left or right leading to points in the valleys where rivers could easily be forded. The ridgeway section, still a passable track today, affords beautiful views of Wiltshire and Dorset before it drops down at White Sheet Hill to join the valley route from Salisbury to Shaftesbury. Before Shaftesbury the upper and lower roads to Blandford (via Melbury Abbas and Cann respectively) are marked, plus an additional road to Blandford from Higher Coomb, which is no longer a through road. Shaftesbury itself has only one branch road marked, to Hindon ('Hendon' on the map).

In reality, Shaftesbury, being an ancient town of major importance, has more roads radiating out of it than any other town in Dorset. Before Ogilby's day, the main route westwards out of Shaftesbury would have been down Tout Hill, around Castle Hill and south of Duncliffe Hill. On Ogilby's map the Sherborne Causeway is used, but the link from Shaftesbury to the Sherborne Causeway through Long Cross was a later construction, providing more-or-less the route we know today. From the Causeway Ogilby's route is much the same, with one noticeable deviation just before Milborne Port, where Ogilby's road takes a more northerly course, from Toomer Hill past Gospel Ash Farm.

Ogilby's folio volume was intended to be the first of three. Unfortunately, he died in the year of publication, and the remaining two volumes were never completed. Nonetheless, the volume that was published was a remarkable achievement and served as a source of reference for publishers for many years to come. Ogilby established the use of the 'statute mile' of 1760 yards (introduced by Act of Parliament in 1593), dispensing with the confusion caused by the use of local or 'customary' miles, which varied in length from 2035 to 2500 yards.

From the moment it appeared, the atlas was in great demand. Two further impressions were published in 1675 and a final one in 1698. Except for the original edition, all maps are numbered in the lower right hand corner from 1 to 100. Because of its unwieldy size (the example illustrated measures 440 mm x 320 mm) and weight (over two kilograms), the atlas was far from being an ideal travelling companion, unless you were in a private coach, so it is surprising that nearly forty-five years elapsed before map-makers attempted to produce a handier version.

However, in 1719, two pocket-sized reductions of the Ogilby atlas appeared from two different publishers, John Senex and

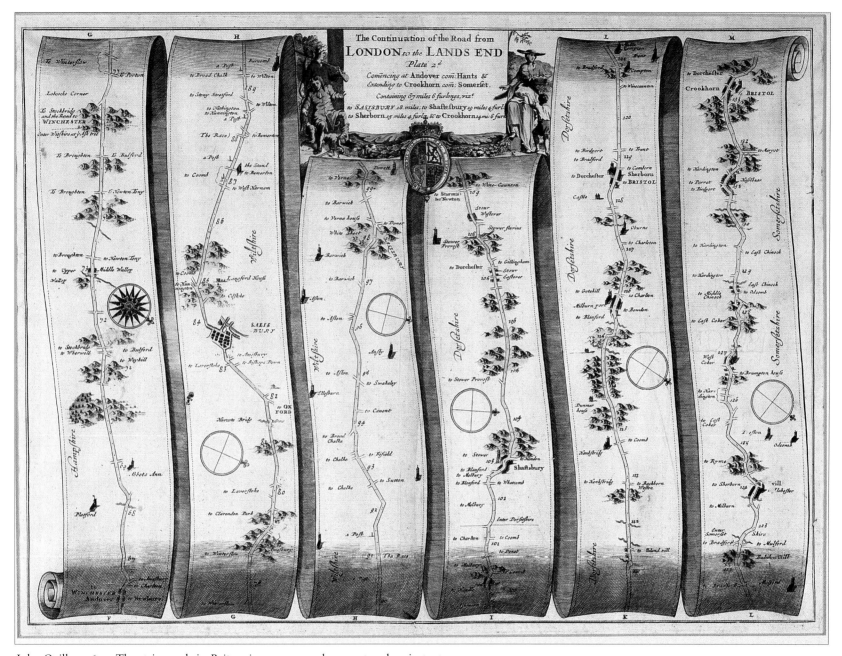

John Ogilby, 1675. The strip roads in *Britannia* were a novel concept and an instant success.

Thomas Gardner. Claims by Senex that *An Actual survey of all the principal Roads of England and Wales* was a 'much improved and corrected' version of Ogilby do not stand up to close inspection. Gardner, on the other hand, made no such claims about his *Pocket Guide to the English Traveller*, whose darkly hatched borders between the strips bear a closer resemblance to Ogilby's and are certainly more attractive than the plainer ones of Senex. The example illustrated, from a later

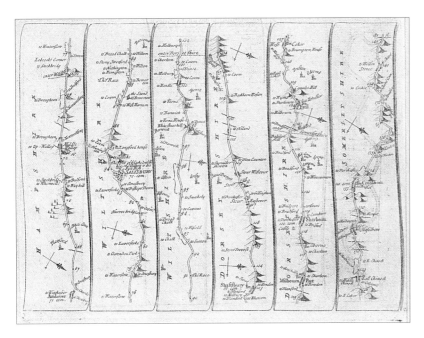

John Senex's reduction of John Ogilby's map; a much handier version for the traveller which went into many editions.

The King of Diamonds from William Redmayne's pack of playing cards, and the Seven of Diamonds from the pack by Robert Morden.

double-sided edition of Senex's atlas, is identical to the one in his 1719 first edition. It shows much the same section of the road from London to Lands End as on Ogilby's, but is distinctive for its compact measurements of 210 mm x 155 mm, being approximately one quarter of the size of Ogilby's map.

WILLIAM REDMAYNE, 1676

Though published in the same year (1676) and similar in size (about 90 mm x 50 mm), the Redmayne playing card is different in many ways from its Morden counterpart. The first difference is its lack of accuracy. Poole Harbour is enlarged out of all proportion, and Dorchester, although more or less correctly placed in relation to the rest of the county, lies on a river (meant to be the Frome), which flows into the sea somewhere in the vicinity of Weymouth, instead of Poole Harbour.

However, the diamond suit filling most of the central part of the county ensured that cartographical exactitude was unlikely to have been the prime object of the publisher, who was more concerned with providing ornament. Of the 'sheepe' mentioned

in the text, four are dotted about in the eastern regions. There are two ships sailing off the coast. The engraver seems to have enjoyed his depiction of the 'merry monarch', Charles II, who is shown crowned and holding his sceptre.

The quaint wording on the card is worth reproducing in full. 'Dorcet-shire Is bounded on the East with Hamp-shire, on the West with Devon-shire, on the South with the Brittish Ocean, and on the North with Wilt-shire & SomersetSh. Its a fertile soil full of Woods and Forrests, store of Sheepe, Dorchester is the chief-Towne in it with Ruind Walls by the Danes. In it are 248 Parrishes and Divers Rivers.'

Redmayne published two editions in 1676, the second set being a newly engraved set, making it fairly easy to identify. This one, from the second edition, has vertical hatching for the red suits, following the usual code of heraldic colouring, whereas in the first edition the suits were engraved in outline and the colour was blocked in, probably stencilled. In the second edition the black suits were 'cross-hatched', also according to the heraldic code. The second edition had its cost reduced from one shilling per pack to sixpence, no doubt in order to stay in competition with the Morden playing cards.

Morden's cards were the first to show roads on a county map of Dorset – too small to be of any real practical use, but breaking important new ground. The West Road through the north of the county is given the greatest prominence with a double line. The other roads, engraved with a single line, radiate out from Blandford to (clockwise) Sherborne, Shaftesbury, Wimborne and Dorchester/Bridport. That there is no sign of the well-established road from Blandford to Salisbury through Cranborne serves to confirm how major a route the West Road was at the time.

During the Civil War, the output of playing cards was severely curtailed, because the pastime was considered sinful by the Cromwellians. Many fine sets of cards were destroyed. They were succeeded by educational packs such as these, containing instruction in history, geography and similar subjects. These novelty cards became popular and are now keenly collected.

JOHN SELLER, 1695

Maps by John Seller are compact and attractive. His most important work, *Anglia Contracta*, a sixty-six map atlas of the counties of England and Wales, was published in 1695. The map illustrated (see page 34), measuring 145 mm x 115 mm, is a reworking of the plate almost a century later by Francis Grose in his fine four volume work published between 1777 and 1787. Entitled *Supplement to the Antiquities of England and Wales*, it contained fifty-two county maps and numerous views of cathedrals, churches, abbeys, castles and ancient remains. Very little is changed from the original plate, apart from the deletion of Seller's name inside the cartouche.

The new element is the descriptive text below the map, a dry catalogue of facts, which continues on the reverse. The compass rose and the grid are retained from Seller's plates. The grid is noteworthy in that it is not a reference to latitude and longitude, but an indication of distance in miles from London (miles south on the vertical axis and miles west on the horizontal axis), an innovation introduced by John Norden, a contemporary of Saxton's.

Seller was a prolific seventeenth century cartographer, who had a remarkable impact on map-making. His principal study was hydrography, and the earliest work attributed to him was *Practical Navigation*, published in 1669. He was appointed official hydrographer to no less than three monarchs – Charles II, James II and Queen Anne. In 1671, the date of publication of his pioneering work *The English Pilot*, he was granted the 'special copyright privilege' by King Charles II, protecting the sales of his atlases and charts for a period of thirty years.

ROBERT MORDEN, 1695

It is not always easy to put one's finger on what exactly makes a map popular with collectors, but in the case of the first example by Robert Morden, published in 1695 (see page 35), it must be a combination of clear engraving, good size, pleasing original colouring and affordability. Measuring 420 mm x 360 mm, it has a decorative cartouche in shades of red, green and yellow.

The boundaries of the hundreds and of the county are highlighted in similar colours. The yellow border carries markings of Longitude in 'Minuits of Time' at the top and 'Degrees' at the bottom, measured (for the first time by any map-maker) from the Meridian of St. Paul's Cathedral. There are no roads on this particular map, although roads are to be found in

The 'miniature' Morden of 1720.

some 1695 editions, for example the one in the Bodleian Library. Maps from the other three editions (1722, 1753 and 1772) all show roads and are difficult to tell apart, although a fine watermark of a parading horse distinguishes maps from the 1722 edition.

Another factor affecting demand is rarity. The second example of Morden's work is a scarce smaller map of Dorset, known as a 'miniature Morden', measuring 210 mm x 175 mm. It first appeared in *The New Description and State of England* in 1701, published jointly by Morden with Thomas Cockeril and Ralph Smith. The identical map appeared again in 1720 in a small edition of *Camden's Britannia*, edited by the Rev. Thomas Cox, called *Magna Britannia et Hibernia*, and it is from this that the illustration is taken. The 1701 edition was the fourth time that a map of the county had shown roads, but (leaving aside Morden's 1695 map, which appeared in too large a volume to be considered as portable) it was the first to be of any practical use to the traveller, unlike Morden's playing card map (which was too small) and Philip Lea's re-issue of Saxton's map in 1690 (which was too large and was also out-of-date).

The miniature Morden is a clear map showing the West Road from London to Sherborne via Shaftesbury; the roads from Weymouth to Bristol and from Poole to Oxford; and the two mail coach roads, from London to Dorchester, and London to Poole via Winchester and Ringwood. Surprisingly, the road from Wimborne to Cranborne is shown crossing the River Allen somewhere between Witchampton and Hinton Martell, whereas other maps until John Cary (see page 64) show it crossing downstream at Little Hinton. I am not aware that the road ever followed the more northerly course.

Cox's *Magna Britannia* also contains a distance table, which is an enlargement of Thomas Jenner's, published nearly eighty years earlier (see page 25). It is attractively coloured and depicts the coats-of-arms of Dorchester, Poole, Lyme Regis, Weymouth, Bridport, Shaftesbury, Wareham and Corfe Castle.

The Morden map of 1695 appeared in a new edition of *Camden's Britannia*. At this time Morden was a bookseller and publisher, working from premises in London's Cornhill. The work was edited by Dr Edmund Gibson (later Bishop Gibson) and contained fifty maps, mainly of the English counties. Most bear the names of Abel Swale, Awnesham and John Churchill, which, in the case of the Dorset map, are in the lower left-hand corner. They were three highly respected publishers who financed the work and commissioned Morden to provide the maps. The three scales of miles were known as 'Great', 'Middle' and 'Small' miles, representing distances of 2430, 2200 and 1830 yards respectively.

ABOVE: Francis Grose's map printed from John Seller's plate of 1695.
OPPOSITE PAGE: Robert Morden's county map of the same date.

The Eighteenth Century

JOHN OWEN AND EMANUEL BOWEN, 1720

By the 1700s map-makers were producing county maps which for the first time included roads as a normal part of the information; amongst them were those by Emanuel Bowen in *Britannia Depicta, or Ogilby Improv'd*. Such was its success, combined with the failure of its publishers to print sufficient copies, that there were eight editions of *Depicta*, all dated 1720 and published before 1724. Several others appeared later and the final edition was published in 1764.

A number of features contributed to its popularity. The road maps were scaled down from John Ogilby's *Britannia*, published forty-five years earlier in 1675, but as it was cheaper and pocket-sized it was more functional than Ogilby. *Britannia Depicta* contained a series of miniature county maps of England and Wales, and was packed full of information, in tiny copperplate script. One of the most distinguishing characteristics of Emanuel Bowen's maps generally is the 'legends' that appear in every available space on the face of each map. The moving spirit behind this may have been his co-author, the historian John Owen, wanting to show off the immensity of his historical and antiquarian knowledge, knowing that the fineness of Emanuel Bowen's engraving would make this possible. A further saving of space was the unusual back to back engraving of maps or strip roads on both sides of the page, resulting in a handier-sized, slimmer volume. The normal custom was for the backs of most line engraved maps to be left blank, apart from the text.

The county map illustrated (see page 38), published in 1720 and measuring 115 mm x 115 mm including the text underneath, has a decorative and finely engraved cartouche above, containing details of the road from Bristol to Weymouth, with distances in computed and measured miles. Beneath the map

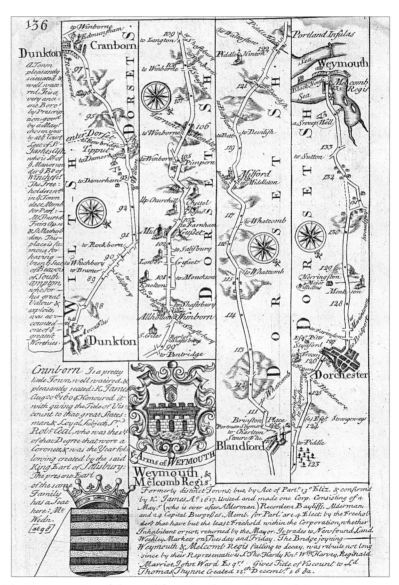

The Dorset section of the road from London to Weymouth in 1720.

appear details of the county, its size, industry and commerce. An earlier page in the atlas (measuring 115 mm x 180 mm) charts the route from London to Weymouth. Scaled down from Ogilby's *Britannia*, the strips contain a wealth of information.

The road enters Dorset in Martin Wood (marked Tipput, a variation on nearby Tidpit, where there is still a milestone giving the distances to Hyde Park Corner and Poole) and continues to Cranborne along the present-day road. From Cranborne to Blandford it follows a very different course from anything that we might recognise today. It goes first to Allhallows Wimborne,

described by Ogilby as a 'discontinued village'. The church is now gone, but nearby stood St. Giles House, the seat of the fourth Earl of Shaftesbury, Lord Lieutenant of Dorset, whose descendent Lord Ashley, the seventh Earl, brought about the humanising Factory Acts in the mid-nineteenth century.

The road then goes through Lower Gusset (Gussage All Saints) and Mid Gusset (Gussage St. Michael), passing between Up Churchill (Long Crichel) and Chettel (Chettle), eventually reaching Tarrant Monkton before crossing high ground (now Blandford Camp) and dropping down into Blandford along,

Emanuel Bowen, 1749. Lighthouses on Portland Bill are shown for the first time.

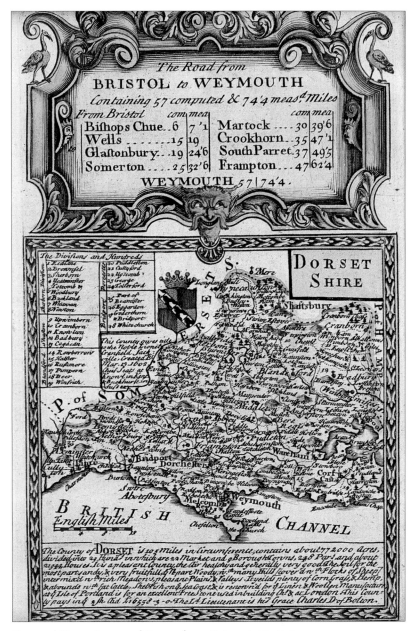

Emanuel Bowen's map of Dorset from *Britannia Depicta*, 1720.

Owen and Bowen's (and Ogilby's) road ran to the south of the existing road, leaving Blandford in the direction of Charlton Marshall, zigzagging its way initially. There followed a straight run to Lower Street (a cluster of farms half a kilometre south of Winterborne Whitechurch) and on to Milford (Milborne St. Andrew), entering the village at an unfamiliar angle. The road continued, much as now, to the top of Basan Hill, but then diverted westwards towards Druce Farm, whereas the present road into Puddletown (incorrectly marked Piddle Hinton) was a later turnpike construction. From Druce Farm it ran through Yellowham Wood and into Dorchester over Stockham (or Stocking) Bridge at Fordington.

The route from Dorchester to Weymouth was much as it is today, except that on Ridgeway Hill it carried straight on into Elwell, turned west into Upwey and then south to Broadwey. Today's more direct road into Broadwey (running parallel with the railway line) is marked with dashed lines and was perhaps either a proposed road or a road under construction, or even a road that had begun to be the favoured route. At the approach to Weymouth near Melcombe Regis there is an interesting symbol marked 'Sweep Well' on the other side of the road from Radipole Lake, near to a windmill. This was a common method of drawing water, as seen elsewhere on this map (on Blackheath Down near Tidpit, also near a windmill).

Another finely engraved map by Emanuel Bowen, published in 1749 and measuring 195 mm x 170 mm, is found in the *Universal Magazine of Knowledge and Pleasure* (see page 37). Like Morden's map from *Magna Britannia* in the previous chapter, it shows the same main roads, this time with post stages marked by crescent moon symbols. Of the many parks in earlier maps, only three now remain: Blagdon, Gillingham and Marshwood. On the edge of the Vale of Whitehart, the anomalous part of Somerset (marked 'f' in the legend on the map) lingers on, looking confusingly like a fourth park.

As far as I am aware this is the first time that lighthouses appear on a county map of Dorset with both the Lower and Higher lighthouses on Portland being indicated. The two lighthouses had been built over thirty years earlier, in 1716, and were needed to give shipping a clear bearing by day and by night past the Bill and the Shambles.

approximately, the existing route from the camp. However, you could look in vain today for many of the sections of this road.

From Blandford to Dorchester the road is equally unfamiliar, since the course of the present A354 was created largely by the Harnham, Blandford and Dorchester Turnpike Trust in 1755-6.

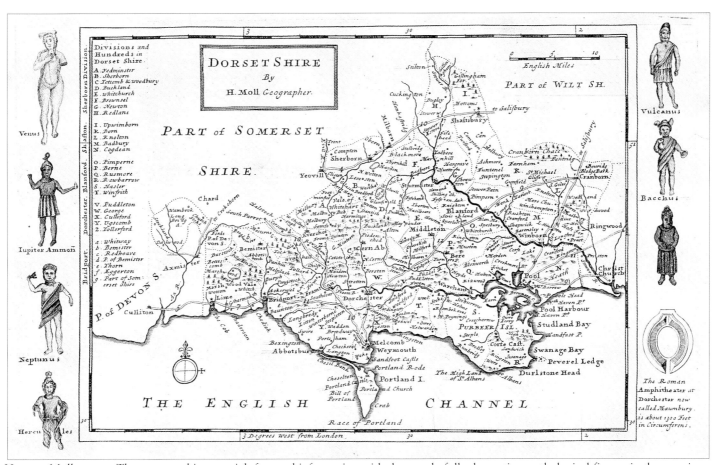

Herman Moll, 1724. The map combines straightforward information with the wonderfully decorative mythological figures in the margin.

HERMAN MOLL, 1724

This attractive map, measuring 255 mm x 180 mm and published in 1724, has some interesting variations compared with its predecessors. The viewer could be forgiven for not recognising many of the place names, which are given some odd spellings by the Dutch cartographer, engraver and publisher, Herman Moll. Who would have recognised Kizwood, Helwarden, Piedenched, Shilling Ok, Fyfpen Auk and Funtenel as being Keysworth, Holworth, Piddletrenthide, Shillingstone, Okeford Fitzpaine and Fontmell Magna? A new spelling of Blagdon appears, Moll designating it as Bladge Park. The height of the cliffs at St. Aldhelm's Head is given curious emphasis by Moll's wording 'The High Land of St. Albans'.

The margins illustrate seven characters from mythology, one of whom remains anonymous. The others are Venus, Jupiter, Neptune, Hercules, Vulcan and Bacchus. The last of the illustrations is the 'Roman Amphitheatre at Dorchester, now called Maumbury'. The hundreds are listed on the left-hand side, divided into groups, with the names of the divisions written sideways in the margin. No doubt for the sake of convenience and legibility, the latitude hatching is omitted beside the names. The conventional signs of asterisks next to towns are used to indicate the number of members returned to Parliament, as are crescent moons for post stages, the latter sign being used here for the first time on a Dorset map.

Ower Ferry too is mentioned for the first time that I am aware of on a Dorset map. When Ower was a principal port for the exporting of stone from Purbeck there was a busy ferry linking it with Brownsea and Poole, which continued to run from Ower Quay long after its heyday. A passage house there, one of a number along the harbour's edge, offered hospitality to travellers and wild-fowlers in the eighteenth and nineteenth centuries.

Though based in The Netherlands, Moll is known to have spent some time working in Britain. He published an atlas of the English and Welsh counties in 1724, calling it *A New Description of England and Wales*, from which this example comes. The atlas was republished in 1740, and again in 1753, but without the archaeological antiquities in the margins, which create such a decorative feature on this example from the first edition.

The county title is displayed in a plain window, unlike the ornamental cartouches found in earlier maps. This reflects the more workmanlike attitude of the age, which was moving towards the Industrial Revolution. Practicality was the order of the day, and this map, showing the principal roads, was intended to be used as a means of reference rather than be seen as a work of art. Following the progress of maps in the eighteenth century, we see less and less fine calligraphy and fewer ornamental cartouches and colourful armorials, which were such an attractive feature of early map-making.

RICHARD WILLIAM SEALE, 1732

Hutchins' *History of Dorset* is widely known as a remarkable work of scholarship, but there is a lesser-known history of Dorset which precedes Hutchins' *History* by some forty-two years. Called a *Survey of Dorsetshire* and published in 1732, the text was plagiarised by the Reverend John Coker from a century-old manuscript of Thomas Gerard, written by the latter in the 1620s. The printer and publisher of the *Survey* was John Wilcox and it contains a frontispiece map, engraved by Richard William Seale.

Measuring 390 mm x 280 mm, it was dedicated to the Honourable George Dodington, who was one of the more colourful characters of the eighteenth century. Squat and unprepossessing, but immensely witty and always lavishly dressed, he was the embodiment of political corruption during the rise of the Whigs in the reigns of George I and II. He lived in the vast mansion of Eastbury House at Tarrant Gunville, inherited from his uncle, who had made his fortune as an army clothing contractor. Despite being born the son of a Weymouth apothecary, George Bubb Dodington's gift for political intrigue was eventually rewarded by achieving his lifelong ambition of being elevated to the peerage, as Lord Melcombe, only to die within a year. What is interesting is that despite the dedication, the map spells Tarrant Gunville incorrectly and does not include Eastbury, although it does include the neighbouring and much smaller Chettle House.

This map has its own character and does not appear to be a copy of previous ones. Blagdon Park is accorded due status, visually, as the largest park in Dorset (1040 acres). Note that it will be over twenty years before the new turnpike road (1755-6) from Blandford to Salisbury via Chettle and Woodyates is created, and another decade before a Dorset map (Isaac Taylor's 1765 large-scale map) will chart the familiar course of this main road, instead of the centuries-old more southerly route. The latter route passes through the ancient ribbon-making market town of Cranborne, where the courts administering the Chase Law were centred and where there was a small priory. Until the Dissolution of the Monasteries the ecclesiastical authorities were largely responsible for maintaining roads, hence medieval routes tended to lead to religious houses such as abbeys, monasteries and priories, which were the hub of the surrounding district.

Seale was a prolific engraver involved in the production of many maps and plans, including this map of Dorset, specifically engraved for Wilcox's brief *Survey*. Rather like the rivers it mentions, the book meanders through descriptions of the county and its principal families, tailing off brusquely with this final paragraph: 'Not farre from Clifton the River Ivell entereth into Somersetshire, whither I meane not to followe it.'

A redeeming feature is the extremely comprehensive and well-indexed collection of Dorset family armorials. There are six pages of them, beautifully engraved, 312 in all.

Richard William Seale, 1732.

THOMAS BADESLADE AND
WILLIAM TOMS, 1742

This unusual map of Dorset, measuring 145 mm x 140 mm, comes from a pocket-size atlas, published in 1742, called *Chorographia Britanniae*. It contains a set of maps of all the counties in England and Wales, as well as four introductory maps, showing, respectively, 'the Sea Coast with the Fortifications, Royal Docks, Harbours, Sands etc.'; 'the Counties with the County Towns'; 'the Great Roads from London to all parts of SOUTH BRITAIN'; and 'a Map of the principal Cross-Roads from one Great Town, to another'. There are detailed distance tables and, at the back of the atlas, an alphabetical list of all the 'Cities, Boroughs and Market Towns'.

The verbose preamble states: 'This Collection (conveying a more comprehensive Idea of South Britain than any thing hitherto publish'd) was first Drawn and compiled into a Pocket Book, by Order and for the Use of his late Majesty KING GEORGE I. By Thomas Badeslade Surveyor and Engineer, and now neatly Engrav'd by Will: Henry Toms.'

The claim that the atlas was 'more comprehensive' seems to be justified. The forty-two county maps are engraved to a high standard, detailing all towns and important villages, together with roads and rivers. The 'forked lightning' effect for rivers persists from sixteenth and seventeenth century cartography, as do the 'molehills' for uplands. Following a pattern set in the Owen and Bowen maps twenty years earlier, the county title is placed outside the printed border.

A compass rose is positioned on the lightly stippled area to the north of the county. A strip of darker shading around the boundary has the effect of throwing the county into relief. The sea, by contrast, is left completely blank, except for shoreline ripples, a new cartographical convention, which carried on into the nineteenth century.

To the left of each map, within the printed border, there is a column of information giving the number of members returned to Parliament (shown with asterisks on the map), the number of boroughs, market towns and parishes, and the market days and fairs. Included in the list is Woodbury Hill Fair, near Bere Regis, once Dorset's largest annual fair. Spread over 5 days, each day

Thomas Badeslade and William Toms, 1742. The text to the left of the map lists the number of MPs for each constituency; the number of boroughs, market towns and parishes; and – perhaps most interestingly – the market days and fairs, only a handful of which still endure.

had its own speciality: Wholesale Day, Gentlefolks' Day, All Folks' Day, Sheep Fair Day (on which cattle and other livestock were also sold) and Pack and Penny Day (cheap offers before the fair closed). This fair was the original of Greenhill Fair in *Far from the Madding Crowd*. It drew folk from all over the county, but as the railways spread, cheap excursions enticed people to travel to other points of interest further afield. Gradually the fair reduced its number of days, until the effect of two World Wars finally forced its closure.

Eighteenth century England was effectively a 'squirearchy'. As far as representation in Parliament was concerned, since the 'Glorious Revolution' in 1688 and the limiting of the powers of the king, Members of Parliament were from this ruling class.

Wealthy landed gentry or sons of newly-rich businessmen could serve the nation in Parliament and locally as Justices of the Peace. Dorset had great estates and thriving trade, so a disproportionate number of Members (20) were returned to Parliament compared with the relatively small population of the county. This imbalance would finally be corrected by the Great Reform Act of 1832, which provided for a substantial redistribution of seats (see pages 89-90).

Until 1832 the types of franchise varied considerably. The members for Lyme Regis and Poole were voted for by the Freemen of their Boroughs. The members for Shaftesbury, Bridport, Dorchester, Wareham and Corfe Castle were 'Scot and lot' (voted for by ratepayers). The four members for Weymouth-Melcombe Regis and the two Dorset County Members were 'Forty-shilling Freeholders' (voted for by freeholder occupiers).

The roads marked on the map hold no surprises, since they have either been shown on previous maps or they are depictions of ancient roads already known to be in existence, but not marked on previous maps.

I believe that this is the first map of the county to show Dorchester's distance from London alongside its name. However, since a standard length of a mile had not yet been adopted by all map-makers, the 97 miles mentioned is a considerable underestimate compared with the county town's distance of 127 miles from London on Owen and Bowen's strip-road map dealt with in a previous chapter. Owen and Bowen's distances were based on John Ogilby's statute mile of 1760 yards, just as Senex and Gardner's distances were also based on Ogilby.

It would be reasonable to suppose that 127 miles from London to Dorchester should correspond with today's measurement. Indeed, when you consult a distance table in a modern road atlas, you find that Dorchester is listed as being 129 miles from London, only two miles different from a calculation made nearly three centuries earlier.

All forty-six maps in the first edition of *Chorographia Britanniae* are dated 1741. There were several re-issues, with a second edition in 1745, and a final one in 1747. Because of the limited number of printings and the high mortality rate of pocket atlases, individual maps are hard to come by.

ROBERT DODSLEY AND JOHN COWLEY, 1744

Robert Dodsley was already a successful writer, poet and publisher, before he ventured into the world of cartography as a bookseller, in 1735. Nine years later, in 1744, he published his first major work, *The Geography of England*. The maps were prepared by John Cowley, 'geographer to his Majesty'. There were fifty-two separate maps of the counties of England and Wales, as well as a map of the whole of England and Wales, a sea chart, a road map and a plan of London. Each map was accompanied by a descriptive text.

As you can see from the example illustrated, which is from *The Geography* and measures 180 mm x 130 mm, the maps themselves are agreeably free of the clutter of place names that seems to typify many eighteenth century maps, especially those from the hand of Emanuel Bowen. At first sight, its claim to be an 'improved map' seems a bit far-fetched in view of the paucity of information. However, it sets out to do no more than to show

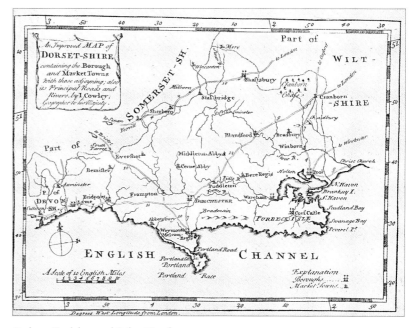

Robert Dodsley and John Cowley, 1744.

the Borough and Market Towns (not necessarily on main roads), and the Principal Roads and Rivers. It achieves its aim. From a traveller's point of view, the roads are extremely clear because of the lack of crowding of place names, and you get the clearest picture so far on any map produced of how the roads and rivers interrelate. The coastline however is extraordinarily erratic.

Because there are so few place names on Cowley's map, it highlights their contemporary importance, though it is a surprise to see such a tiny place as Chalbury (spelt Chadbury) given a mention. Some, such as Cerne Abbas and Milton Abbas (reverting here to the older name of Middleton) are well known for their former abbeys and priories and it is not too surprising that they have hung on to their status. Others we might not have realised had been important in their day, such as Beaminster, Evershot and Bradbury (a misspelling of Badbury). Evershot, formerly a small market town, continued to have a certain status owing to its proximity to the Earl of Ilchester's Melbury estate. Its status was further enhanced in 1628, when Christopher Stickland of Yealdon, Bedfordshire, founded a Free School in the place of his birth, by deed of charity. This charitable gentleman granted to trustees a farm in Over Kentcombe in the parish of Toller Porcorum, whose rent would provide for 'the yearly stipend and maintenance of some honest painful and sufficient learned schoolmaster yearly and successively for ever.'

Often a town's prosperity was based on manufacture. Most Dorset towns in the seventeenth century produced cloth. Sailcloth was made at Beaminster, serge at Winterborne Stickland and linen at Burton Bradstock, where sailcloth was also made. In the eighteenth century 'swan's-skin', a warm flannel for soldiers, sailors and Newfoundland fishermen, was produced in Shaftesbury. In the early 1750s a silk factory was established in Sherborne, and silk was also manufactured in Cerne Abbas, Gillingham and Stalbridge. The raw material for these products (apart from silk) was either hemp or flax, which at one time were grown all over Dorset. Both had a wide range of uses and were made into canvas, linen, nets, oil, food, lighting, carpets, tow, paper, clothing, twine, thread and tools.

Many of the industries mentioned above were wiped out by the Industrial Revolution. Cheap steam power from coal led to the rise of the textile industry in the north, and Dorset, with no coal,

fell by the wayside. Nonetheless, some survived into the nineteenth century. Glove-making continued in Beaminster, Blandford, Gillingham and Sherborne; so did another cottage industry – button-making – in Blandford, Bere Regis and Shaftesbury. By the mid-eighteenth century Abraham Case's grandson, Peter, had brought the button-making business to new heights with the aid of an astute Yorkshire businessman, John Clayton, who reorganised the company. Not only were more than 700 workers now employed within the industry, but a sales and marketing office was established in London and an export branch was opened in Liverpool. Additional depots were set up in Sixpenny Handley, Milborne Stileham (now part of Milborne St. Andrew), Piddletrenthide, Langton Matravers and Wool. In 1781 another depot was created in Lytchett Minster in what is now the Old Button Shop.

Cowley's identical maps were reissued in 1745 (one year after The Geography of England) in another atlas entitled A New Set of Pocket Maps of all the counties of England and Wales. The Dodsley and Cowley enterprise endured successfully for many years. From 1755 to 1764, Robert Dodsley took his younger brother James into partnership. The two of them published Thomas Kitchin's England Illustrated in 1764. After 1764, James Dodsley continued the business in his own name. The final flourishing of the Dodsley name occurred in 1770, when maps from England Illustrated were used in James Dodsley's last cartographic publication, Kitchin's English Atlas.

THOMAS AND JOHN OSBORNE, 1748

Thomas and John Osborne were publishers whose main work was a pocket atlas entitled Geographia Magnae Britanniae. There were only two editions, in 1748 and 1750, containing sixty-three small maps of the counties of England, Wales and Scotland. Each map is numbered (Dorset is number 10) and each starts with the title 'A Correct Map of . . .'. They were engraved by Thomas Hutchinson. The atlas included maps of the Channel Islands, the Isle of Man and the Scilly Isles.

The map of Dorset, measuring 170 mm x 145 mm and from the first edition, is very clearly engraved, like all the others in the series, and shows roads as well as important towns and villages.

Thomas and John Osborne, 1748; one of the last maps to show the old system of roads prior to the creation of turnpikes.

The hilly regions are depicted with the 'molehills' favoured by Saxton's engravers. The county title is set in a carefully engraved representation of a picture frame. The scale of miles and the unexpectedly ornate compass rose are the only other embellishments on this delightfully simple map. Another noteworthy economy is the simple use of the wording 'The Channel'.

Published just before the spate of turnpike roads from 1750 – 1780, it is one of the last maps to show the old system of roads, and is particularly comprehensive, especially for so small a map. The only road of any significance omitted is the link from Weymouth to Wyke Regis, shown six years earlier on Badeslade and Toms' map. Note that the Isle of Purbeck is empty of roads and place names, and that Brownsea Island has been left out altogether – presumably because it got in the way of the lettering for Poole Harbour – which, like the town, is here spelled correctly for the first time.

The turnpike trusts were set up (around twenty in Dorset) in order to develop an improved and more comprehensive road system. Prominent local people would apply for an Act of Parliament allowing them to set up a turnpike in return for constructing and maintaining a section of road and charging a toll, thus earning interest on the capital which had been raised by subscription. The needs of the people of Dorset were well served by this system for around a hundred years until the abolition of the turnpike roads between 1860 and 1888, after which time all main roads became the responsibility of the new county councils.

The turnpike system was an inevitable consequence of the political events of the latter part of the previous century. The Monmouth Rebellion of 1685 represented the dying gasp of civil war in England. The Glorious Revolution three years later paved the way for more enlightened government, which upheld civil liberties and engendered social advances. In this political climate it was natural that travel should become more widespread and communication more effective.

It was plain, however, that the country's road system was inadequate for the task, relying on maintenance by parishes, which could ill afford to provide the manpower demanded by 'Statute Labour', the system existing since 1555, whereby parishes were compelled to provide, for up to six days annually, either labourers or a cart with two able-bodied men, under the supervision of a surveyor. With the establishment of the Turnpike Trusts by Act of Parliament, not only was the maintenance of long stretches of road controlled by a single local organisation, but the capital investment required was repaid by tolls levied on the traffic which used them.

This is a rare map coming at a turning point in road history. It is worth studying closely. Many of the roads shown are within years of falling into disuse or reverting to country lanes. Once crucial hubs like Cranborne and Milton Abbas are on the brink of their long decline, as the turnpikes carved new routes across the county, creating the network of major and minor roads that are still in use today.

Examples from the atlas are quite scarce, probably because the editions were small (a few hundred). One wonders what the financial returns were for the comparatively large number of publishers who joined Thomas Osborne in the venture, for the title page carries the names of no less than seven other publishers.

THOMAS KITCHIN AND THOMAS JEFFERYS, 1749

In 1749 Thomas Kitchin and Thomas Jefferys published their *Small English Atlas* containing fifty maps of the counties of England and Wales. Maps from *The Small English Atlas* are remarkably similar to those of Badeslade and Toms (see page 42) published seven years earlier in 1742. The example illustrated, which measures 130 mm x 110 mm, breaks new ground by marking the distances between towns. The atlas is also remarkable for its delightfully decorative title page.

Kitchin's contribution to eighteenth century cartography was unparalleled. His output was enormous and he collaborated with nearly all of his famous contemporaries, perhaps the best known of all being Emanuel Bowen. Between 1747 and 1794, his name was linked with no less than thirty publishers and cartographers.

One of the finest of Kitchin's maps is the one illustrated from *The Royal English Atlas*, reissued in 1794 by R. Martin, in a

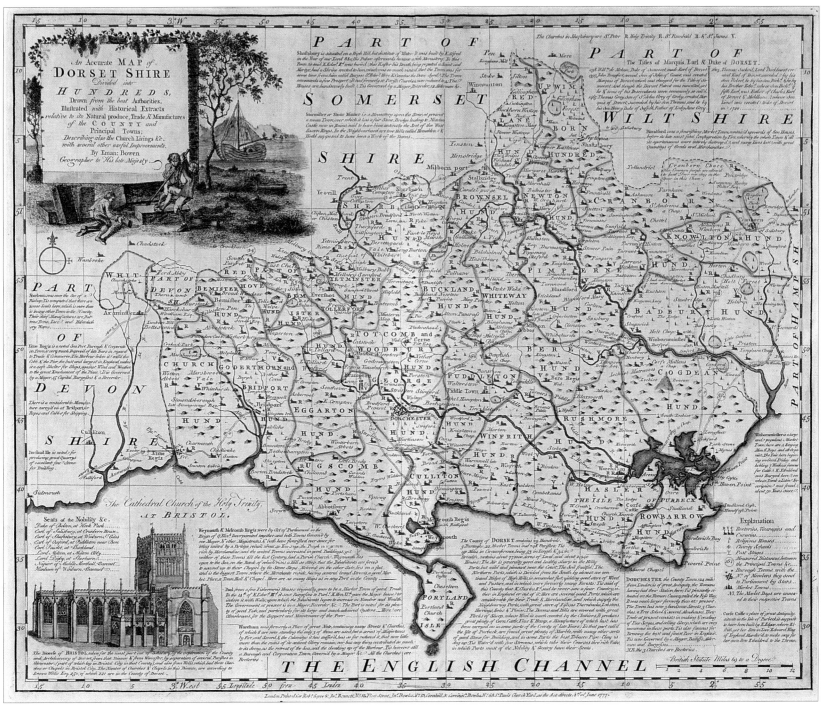

R. Martin's *The English Atlas*, 1794 (but dated 1777), a re-issue of Thomas Kitchin's *The Royal English Atlas*,
and probably the most informative of all single sheet maps of Dorset.

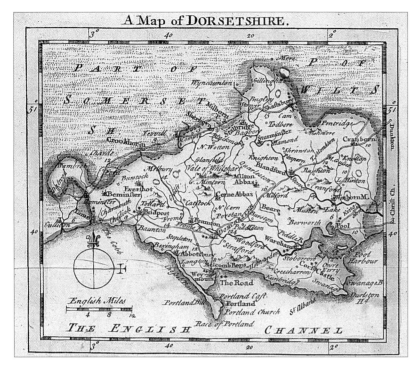

A Map of DORSETSHIRE.

Thomas Kitchin and Thomas Jefferys' map of Dorset, from the *Small English Atlas*, 1749.

work entitled *The English Atlas*. Engraved by Emanuel Bowen, it is a superb example of calligraphic copper engraving of the period. Measuring 500 mm x 405 mm and dated 1777, it has a wealth of detail about the county, engraved in fine copperplate on every available surface, and is probably the most informative single sheet map of Dorset ever produced.

The view around the title cartouche is of quarrymen cleaving blocks of stone on the Isle of Portland. The vignette in the lower left-hand corner is of Bristol Cathedral. The diocese of Bristol, founded in the mid-sixteenth century, took in parishes from the dioceses of Salisbury, Worcester, Gloucester and Wells. The last part of the description records that 'The Number of Churches & Chapels in this Diocese are according to Brown Willis Esq. 250, of which 221 are in the County of Dorset.' In the top right-hand corner it states that 'The Churches in Shaftsbury are St. Peter R, Holy Trinity R, St. Rumbold R & St. James V.' The other churches around the map are also marked R, V or C according to whether the incumbent was a rector, vicar or curate. Religious

Houses are marked with the symbol of a bishop's crozier beside the name of the town in which they were to be found, namely Sherborne, Shaftesbury, Sturminster, Cranborne, Wimborne Minster, Milton Abbas, Cerne Abbas, Wareham, Dorchester, Abbotsbury and Bridport. Charity Schools, signified by a Maltese cross, were located in Sherborne, Stalbridge, Poole, Dorchester, Maiden Newton, Cattistock (spelt Catstock), and Yetminster.

Post stages are marked with the usual crescent moon and boroughs sending Members to Parliament with asterisks, one per Member. Mileages written in a circle on the roads are 'Measured Distances between the Principal Towns etc.' The information on this map is quite dated and all the roads are pre-turnpike. Apart from the 'Explanation' of symbols and the scale of 'British Statute Miles 69 to a Degree', the other descriptions are of the county, its principal towns and its nobility, except for one on 'Cranborn Chace', which records that 'The Common people are allow'd to hunt Deer one day in the Year in this Chace' (this may not be true, as it is not recorded elsewhere).

The description of the county is worth quoting in full:

'The County of DORSET contains 29 Hundreds, 9 Buroughs, 22 Market Towns and 248 Parishes; Tis 150 Miles in Circumference, being 53 in Length & 34 in Breadth, contains about 772000 Acres of Land, and about 21940 Houses: The Air is generally good and healthy, sharp in the Hilly Parts, but mild and pleasant near the Coast; The Soil fruitful; The Northern Parts, which is Divided from the South by almost one continued Ridge of High Hills, is somewhat flat, yielding good store of Wood and Pasture, and in which were formerly many Forests: Tis said of this County that K. Charles II.d said he never saw a finer Country, either in England or out of it: Here are several good Ports, which are considerable for their Trade & Merchandize, and which supply the Neighbouring Parts, with great store of Fish; as Thornbacks, Lobsters, Herrings, Soles and Plaise; The Downs and Hills are covered with great Flocks of Sheep, whose Wool is much coveted by the Clothiers; It produces great plenty of Corn, Cattle, Flax & Hemp, a Manufacture of which last has been carried on in some parts of the County of late Years: In that part call'd the Isle of Purbeck, are found great plenty of Marble, with many other sorts of good Stone for Building, and in some Parts the best Tobacco Pipe Clay is dug up: Tis Water'd with fine Streams, which take their Courses thro' rich Vales, in which Parts most of the Nobility & Gentry have their Seats.'

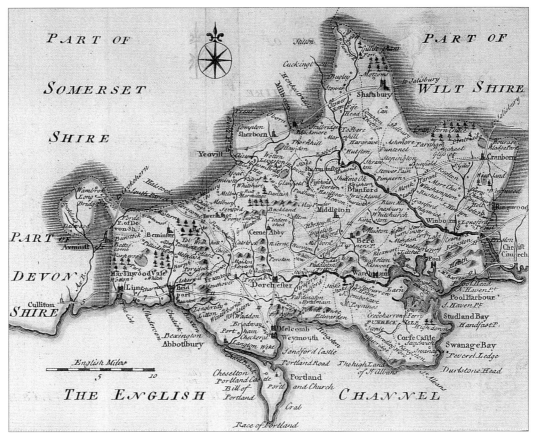

John Rocque, from *The Small British Atlas*, 1753.

The extraordinary thing about the maps from Kitchin's *Royal English Atlas* is that they are potted histories as much as they are maps, even though they are hardly any larger than those of Saxton and Speed nearly two centuries earlier. *The Royal English Atlas* was published in 1762, five years before Emanuel Bowen's death. From 1755 to 1794 the many editions of *The Royal English Atlas* and *The Large English Atlas* were published by all the famous names of the day. The maps in *The English Atlas* are all dated 1777 or 1778, and were engraved by either Emanuel Bowen or Thomas Kitchin, with the exception of two (Middlesex and Surrey), which were engraved by Thomas Bowen. And there you have the key to the quality. Those three names – Thomas Kitchin, Thomas Bowen and Emanuel Bowen – were the central figures in the development and expansion of map-making in Britain during the eighteenth century.

JOHN ROCQUE, 1753

John Rocque was of Huguenot origin and settled in England as a young man in about 1735. He quickly established himself as a leading surveyor, engraver and publisher, and soon afterwards he was appointed Topographer to the Prince of Wales. His French extraction is reflected in the sub-title of the most important atlas he produced, *The Small British Atlas*, or *Le Petit Atlas Britannique*, published in 1753 by Rocque and Sayer (possibly the most prolific cartographic publishers of the eighteenth century).

The forty-six maps in this work were first published by Rocque in his three volume *English Traveller* in 1746. The maps are identical, and the county boundaries have a distinctive heavy shading, giving the county the appearance of an island. Measuring 192 mm x 152 mm, the Dorset example has the bold title DORSET-SHIRE outside the border at the head of the map and the lack of adornment gives it an attractive appearance. The hand-colouring has been quite sensitively done, using green and yellow for the county boundary, red for the towns and for the alternate segments of the scale of miles, and blue for the sea coast and main rivers. As is sometimes the case on early Dorset maps, Portland Bill and Chesil Beach are shown as separate from the mainland, emphasising Portland's insular state.

The marking of Portland Church is of interest, because the next time that it appears on a county map (Isaac Taylor's large-scale map of 1765, page 54) it is referred to as Old Portland Church. For some time St. Andrew's precarious position on the edge of the cliff had been causing concern to the inhabitants, mainly because erosion had caused enormous fissures to open up.

Thomas Gerard wrote in 1625 that 'for Safetie of it they have been forced to wall the Church Yarde Bankes almost of an incredible Height, soe that it afrighte one to look downe.' The wall was effective, but huge landslips from the east side of Portland in 1665 and 1734 invoked fresh fears and special levies ('Every Beast to pay 3d and every twenty sheep 6d').

In 1753, the date of publication of Rocque's map, a committee was formed and a decision made to erect a new church on a different site. Local architect and builder Thomas Gilbert was commissioned to produce the plans, which showed the influence of Sir Christopher Wren, who had employed Gilbert's grandfather as a quarry agent seventy years earlier. An Act of Parliament was passed in 1755 providing the necessary powers to abandon the old church, raise funds, acquire a site and sell pew seats. An appeal had already been launched and George II, who had been petitioned, generously donated £500. Completed in 1766, the church in Reforne was named St. George's (appropriately in view of its royal benefactor) and was consecrated by the Bishop of Bristol in whose diocese it was situated.

Ironically it was the pew seats, whose revenue had helped to finance the church, that proved to be its undoing some 150 years later. The Act of Parliament required pew owners to keep theirs in good repair, but as the years went by this became impossible to enforce, as families dispersed. Disused since 1917, St. George's was restored to its former splendour in the 1970s, and is now regarded as one of the most important examples of Georgian architecture in Dorset.

Subsequent editions of Rocque's atlas were published in 1762 (the year of his death), in 1764, and in 1769 with a new title *England Displayed*. After Rocque's death, the business was taken over by his wife, Mary Ann, who under her name published some of her husband's works until 1775, the last date on which the name Rocque appears in the cartographic business.

GEORGE BICKHAM, 1754

George Bickham, renowned for the quality of his engraving, produced bird's-eye views of the various counties intended to be companions to the illustrations in his *British Monarchy*, published in 1754. The Dorset example dates from 1750, measuring 140 mm x 225 mm, with its accompanying pages of text beautifully engraved on copper-plate, rather than type-set.

The view (see opposite page) is a fanciful glimpse into the heartlands of Dorset from the mouth of the River Stour. The eye is drawn into the folds of the landscape in the search for familiar landmarks and places. The swirling cumulus gives a further look of grandeur to a remarkable scene, which is absolutely in keeping with the spirit of the age. The great landscape gardeners such as Capability Brown and William Kent were designing 'to order' for the owners of stately homes, who wanted the 'picturesque'. In essence, this meant providing an artificially wild and untamed landscape, which could then be civilised and tamed by a cultured Georgian age. Irregularity was the keynote and the extremes of formality prevalent at the turn of the century gave way to a romanticised view of nature. By the middle of the century the romantic revival was complete and the picturesque style with grottoes, Gothic ruins and classical temples was the height of fashion.

In this scene, the craggy cliff in the foreground overlooking the Stour is Hengistbury Head, Milton Abbas is overshadowed by the rough outcrops of Bulbarrow and in the background the view is dominated by lowering Beaminster Down and Batcombe Hill. More easily identifiable are the features along the coast, which are reasonably true to the actual topography, if not to scale. Appropriately, the county town is central to the scene. A charming touch is the wording on the road in the foreground, which lets us into a secret, whence came the coach trotting into view: 'From the Crown Inn Dorchester'.

ISAAC TAYLOR, 1765

Isaac Taylor (1730-1807) was the first map-maker to produce a large-scale survey of the county, contributing more than any other single map to Dorset road history. Measuring 1550 mm x 1130 mm, or nearly 6 by 4 feet, it was published in 1765, and was the direct result of a Royal Society of Arts' advertisement in 1759, which offered 'to give a sum not exceeding £100 as a gratuity to any person . . . who shall make an accurate survey of any county upon the scale of one inch to one mile; the sea coasts of all maritime counties to be correctly laid down, together with

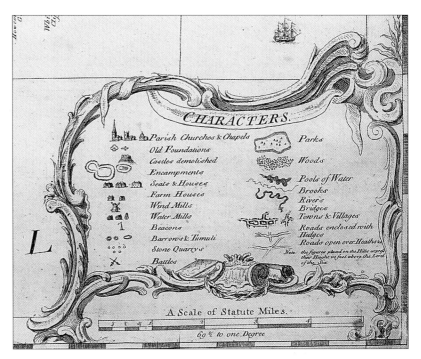

ABOVE. A decorative cartouche contains the 'Characters', which we would refer to today as 'conventional signs'. A recent innovation (found in Kitchin's 1762 *Royal English Atlas*) was the naming of the owners of the 'Seats & Houses' on the map itself and we are able to see the contemporary residents of the stately homes of Dorset. For those not familiar with surveyed elevations, a note is added: 'the figures placed on the Hills express their Height in feet above the Level of the Sea.' The shading of the hills gives an impression of gradient, as found on Cary's maps and the earliest Ordnance Survey. This would lead ultimately to contour lines.

OPPOSITE PAGE. To the north of Blandford, near Stourpaine Bushes, a row of tents is marked 'Camp in 1756'. In this year the Seven Years' War began and from this camp General Wolfe's soldiers prepared to scale the Heights of Abraham by practising at nearby Hambledon Hill. In spite of its strong position, Wolfe captured Quebec from the French in 1759, but lost his life in the process, aged only 32. Note the two obelisks in the Upper Park at Kingston Lacy (bottom right hand corner). They were erected by Joseph Bankes in the 1730s, but only one still stands.

In 1759 the Royal Society of Arts had issued a challenge to produce an accurate large-scale survey. By dedicating his map to the Earl of Shaftesbury and to twenty-three local gentlemen 'in Gratitude for their generous assistance in this Work,' Isaac Taylor hoped to win the approval of the aristocracy and gentry of Dorset, but the map's many inaccuracies brought criticism from the very stratum of society he imagined would win him support.

their latitudes and longitudes; and they desire that they may be able to procure satisfactory proofs of the merit of such performance, and if any person do propose to make such a survey they are desired to signify their particular intentions.'

Taylor was one of the first surveyors to take up the challenge, but the Society's demands also made him the first person to have

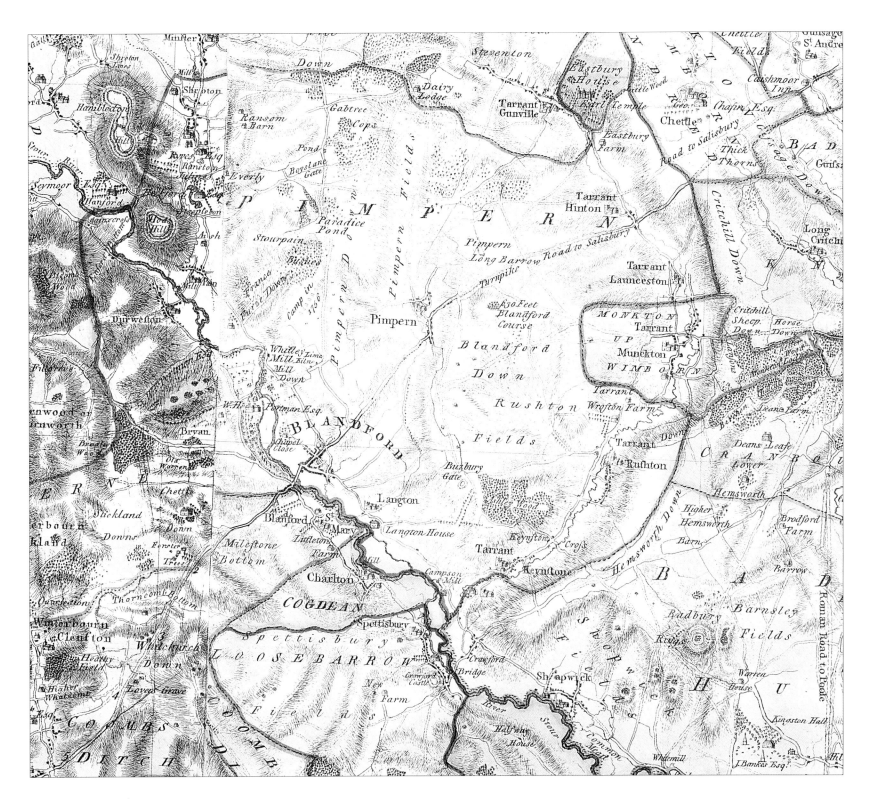

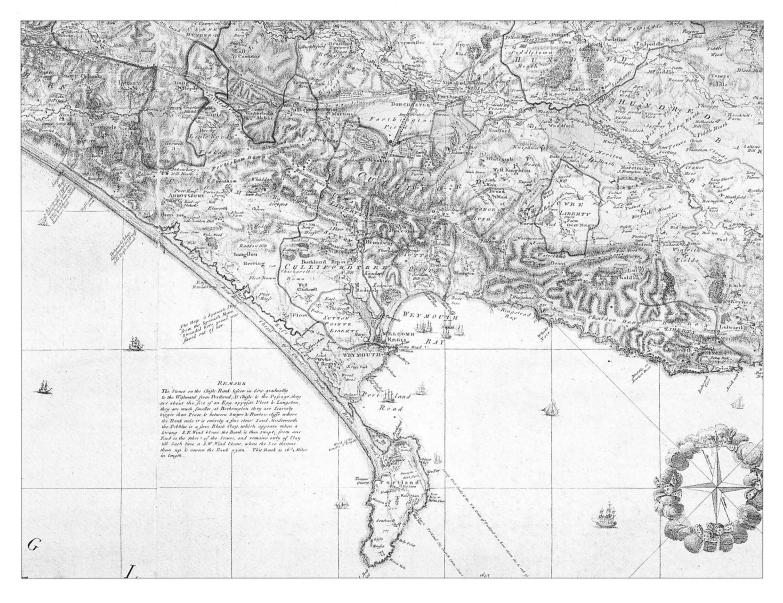

Off Chesil Bank there is a reference to three shipwrecks on the notoriously dangerous beach. In 1748 *The Squirrel*, a tobacco ship, was stranded ('most of the people drowned'). A year later a Spanish ship, *The Hope*, carrying a cargo of bullion was stranded ('here 30,000 pounds was saved out of her'). The third, 'A Logwood Ship, retaken by the *Culloden*, was stranded here [in] 1758 & the boat [was] thrown over the beach on the wall.' If the wind and the sea were driving a ship towards the beach, a skipper's only chance was to set full sail, ride the boat on to the beach and, keeping the sails full, allow the passengers to make their escape. The crew then had to make the best of it at the last minute, for if the sails slackened for a moment, the undertow dragged the boat beneath the waves and all was lost.

a map rejected. Some of his place names were inaccurate (e.g. Hill Halt near Stanbridge should be High Hall) and many of the panels did not match, so some of the roads did not meet where panels joined and the colourists could not follow the boundaries properly. Despite its flaws, Taylor's map remains a remarkable piece of work, and even today is of immense interest to anyone investigating the county's past. The five details I have chosen as illustrations cannot hope to do it justice, but they give a little of its flavour and show Taylor's astonishing eye for detail.

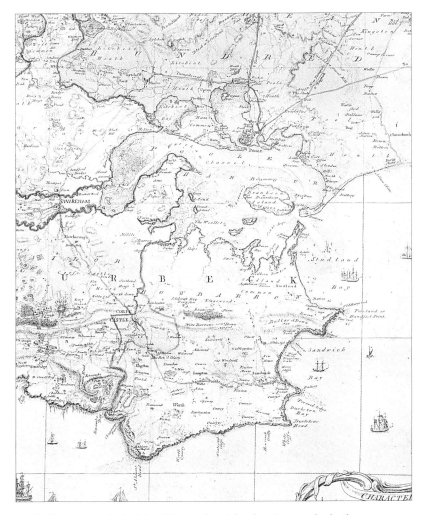

Poole Harbour and the Isle of Purbeck, with what is now the built-up conurbation between Poole and Bournemouth all still shown as heathland. The map was made at exactly the same time as the smuggler Isaac Gulliver was landing contraband along this section of the Dorset coast.

Its greatest importance is what it can tell us about the road system. This is because Taylor not only marks the new turnpikes, but also shows the course of many of the pre-turnpike roads. An example of a new turnpike is the 1755-6 Harnham, Blandford and Dorchester turnpike, which by-passed Cranborne to the north.

Also marked, however, is much of the old Cranborne to Blandford road entering Blandford from the downs. This is the best map that I know of for tracing the path of the old roads of Dorset, even though there are missing links, such as along the pre-turnpike road from Shaftesbury to Sherborne, which used to skirt the south side of Duncliffe Hill on its route through Woodville, Stour Provost and Fifehead Magdalen. The fun is in filling in these gaps in one's imagination, or better still going to see for oneself. Often 'nicks' or 'stubs' (waste triangles of roadside verge) are evidence of a former junction with another road and there the detective work begins.

Another aspect of Taylor's map which is of great value to the naturalist is that there are at least two hundred identifiable woods. That he took the trouble to survey the county with such attention to detail does him great credit, but more significant is the fact that his map depicted the county as it was before the rich man's vogue for building (or rebuilding) stately homes, reshaping the landscape and planting new woodland gained momentum. The ancient woods on Taylor's map are, therefore, a unique glimpse into the past, represented for the last time before they are subsumed into a vastly changed countryside.

It is unlikely that more than a couple of hundred copies of his map would have been issued, and only a few are known to be in existence, but its importance lies in its being the first large-scale survey of the county, later reissued in 1795 by William Faden, who also drew the first Ordnance Survey map.

ESTATE MAPS, 1742, 1773-4, 1799

The first chapter, on the sixteenth century, included Ralph Treswell's survey of the Isle of Purbeck in 1586, an exceptionally early example of an estate map. Others followed, and as Dorset's new breed of landowners consolidated their hold on the countryside, creating estates that reflected their status, more and more of them commissioned estate maps as a practical aid to farming and improving their land. The golden age of the local land surveyor lasted from about 1700 to 1870, when cheap imports and falling land prices heralded the start of an agricultural recession. Enormous numbers of surveys appeared and it is not difficult to pick out examples that reflect their character.

The first I have chosen is part of a Kingston Lacy estate map. Three almost identical maps made up the set, each of them

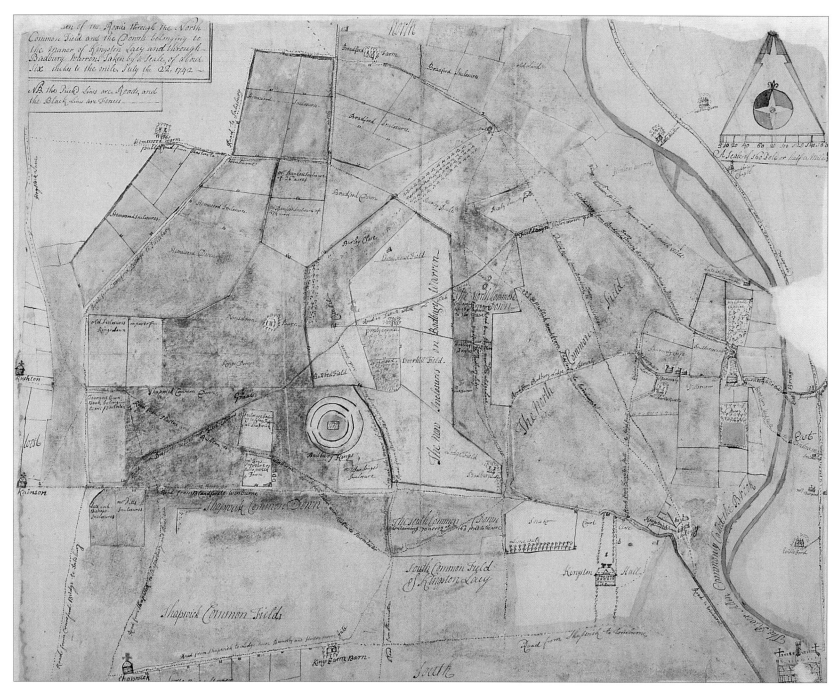

The Kingston Lacy Estate Map of 1742. Kingston Hall is an almost perfect replica of Sir Roger Pratt's mansion of 1663. Note the 'New Inclosures on Badbury Warren', indicating recent enclosure of land.

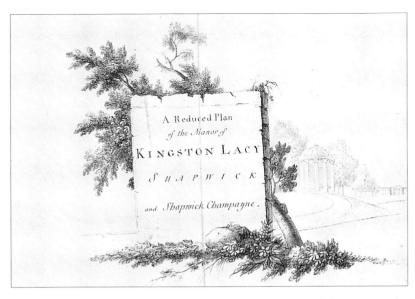

The title page, showing the rotunda, of the 1773-4 *Survey of the Manors of Kingston Lacy, Shapwick, Shapwick Champagne and Tomson.*

During the second half of the eighteenth century, many other Dorset estates were mapped by distinguished surveyors; for example, the Fox-Strangways' Ilchester Estate by Samuel Donne, the Pitt-Rivers Estate by Benjamin Pryce and the Weld Estate at Lulworth by John and Thomas Sparrow.

One of the more unusual estate maps is John Doyley's leather-bound, gold-tooled, 1799 survey of Urles Farm at Corscombe, where the eighteenth century philanthropist and benefactor of Harvard University, Thomas Hollis (1720-1774), retired to enjoy his 3000 acre estate. It was Hollis' fancy to name his farms and fields according to his Whig and Republican sentiments, hence some extraordinary names. Harvard Farm (the map measures 125 mm x 190 mm) has fields named to this day New England, Boston, Massachusetts, Adams, Revolution, William III,

dating from 1742 and measuring approximately 600 mm x 480 mm. Kingston Hall is shown as an almost perfect replica in miniature of the original 1663 mansion designed by Sir Roger Pratt. The nearby Badbury Rings are depicted by three concentric circles with a small rectangle in the centre. There are the traditional dividers and compass rose associated with maps from previous centuries. The title of the map states: 'A Plan of the Roads through the North Common Field and the Downs belonging to the Manor of Kingston Lacy and through Badbury Warren Taken by a Scale of about six inches to the mile July the 22 1742.' Significantly, the wording 'New Inclosures on Badbury Warren' indicates that there had been some recent enclosure of land. Enclosure had been happening from medieval times, first by 'assarting' (permission to bring land into cultivation), then by landlords who wanted to pasture sheep, cattle or even deer instead of allowing the land to remain arable, and finally, from about 1760 onwards, enclosure by Act of Parliament.

A later example of an estate map is the *Survey of the Manors of Kingston Lacy, Shapwick, Shapwick Champagne and Tomson*, made by William Woodward in 1773-4 for Henry Bankes. It can be viewed on microfilm in the Dorset County Record Office, who hold the original for the National Trust.

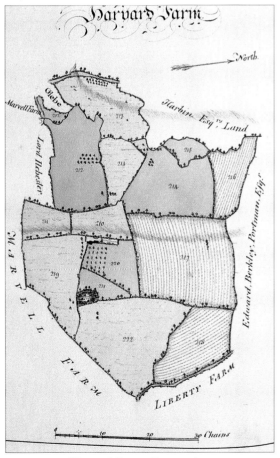

Harvard Farm, Corscombe.

Settlement and Hanover. He named one wood Stuart, so that he could derive anti-Jacobite satisfaction by beheading it every time he coppiced or thinned its trees.

Sadly, this energetic, self-styled 'Assertor of Liberty, Citizen of the World', who described the earth at Urles Farm as 'sweet beyond a nosegay', died quite suddenly in 1774 whilst giving instructions to his farmworkers. Hollis had ordered that his 'corpse be deposited in a grave ten feet deep, and that the field should be immediately ploughed over, that no trace of the burial-place might remain.' His last wishes were followed to the letter and no one knows the exact location of this remarkable man's remains.

JOHN BAYLY, 1773

John Bayly's map of the county was included as the frontispiece in what is undoubtedly the single most important book about Dorset ever to be published, in the 1774 first edition of Hutchins' *History and Antiquities of the County of Dorset.* Measuring 685 mm x 490 mm, it is described as 'A Map of Dorsetshire from Actual Surveys and Records of the County, by J. Bayly, 1773.'

John Hutchins was born in 1698 at Bradford Peverell and was ordained into the Church of England, ultimately becoming rector of Wareham and Swyre. His antiquarian interests led him to begin work on his great *History* in the early 1730s. Encouraged by his patrons, Jacob Bancks and Browne Willis, he had transcribed many folios relating to Dorset, copied from national records then held at the Tower of London and brought back to Wareham in 1761. The following year a disaster occurred and his *History* might never have seen the light of day. Hutchins was away at his parish near Bridport when a great fire swept through Wareham and the rectory was burned to the ground. But for the timely action of his wife, who gathered up his papers and went and stood in the River Frome with 30 years of hard-won scholarship in her arms until help arrived, the unique *History* would have been lost to posterity. Sadly Hutchins died in 1773, the year before his *History* was published, so he never saw his life's work in print.

An unusual feature of this map is the inset in the top left-hand

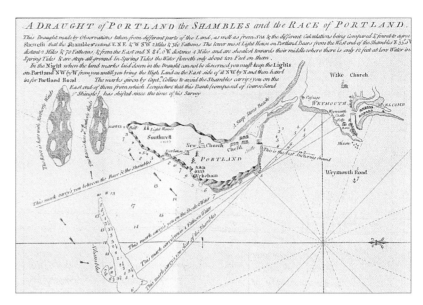

The inset map by John Bayly of the Isle of Portland, from the first edition of John Hutchins' *History of Dorset.*

corner, depicting 'A Draught of Portland, the Shambles and the Race of Portland'. This very detailed chart, showing the Race in northerly and southerly winds, navigable passages and the 'best Anchoring Ground', was reproduced from Captain Greenvile Collins' *Great Britain's Coasting Pilot,* which was published in 1693 and was the first original sea atlas to be produced by an Englishman. Note the windmills on the high ground and the passage house for the ferry from Weymouth to Portland.

When Henry VIII ordered a castle to be built at Weymouth, the local seamen must have been consulted about the position selected for Sandsfoot Castle (marked Weymouth Castle on the map), because it was aligned with the north-east point of the Isle of Portland, allowing 4 fathoms draught over the Shambles, thus providing a sailing mark for a safe navigable bearing across Portland Road into Weymouth.

As we have seen, the first map to show the new turnpike roads was Isaac Taylor's large-scale map in 1765, but a map of this size was expensive, impractical and could only be owned by a wealthy minority. Bayly's 1773 map on the other hand was a handy adjunct to Hutchins' *History* and a good ready-reference for the turnpike roads, none more than twenty years old. 1773 was also the year in which the General Turnpike Act attempted

The Isle of Purbeck and Poole Harbour, from John Bayly's map of 1773.

to combine the innumerable small local trusts into larger units.

Here is a chronological list of turnpike roads created over a twenty-five-year period, during the heyday of the turnpike trusts:

1752-3 Great Western Post Road (or West Road) from London to Exeter and Plymouth via Shaftesbury and Sherborne (Shaftesbury & Sherborne Trust);

1753-4 Bridport to Axminster (Harnham, Blandford & Dorchester Trust);

1755-6 Poole to Salisbury via Wimborne and Cranborne (Poole, Wimborne & Cranborne Trust); Beaminster to Bridport; Bridport to Salisbury via Dorchester and Blandford (the latter called the Great Western Turnpike and the last two administered by the Harnham, Blandford and Dorchester Trust);

1757-8 Lyme Regis to Axminster turnpike (Lyme Regis & Crewkerne Trust);

1758-9 Wimborne to Ringwood (Ringwood, Longham and Leigh Trust);

1760-1 Sherborne to Weymouth via Dorchester; Poole to Sherborne via Blandford and Hazelbury Bryan (both administered by the Weymouth, Melcombe Regis & Dorchester Trust); Ringwood to Great Western Turnpike via Horton Inn (Ringwood, Longham and Leigh Trust);

1764-5 Blandford First and Second District Trusts, formed to take over, respectively, the western part of the Great Western Turnpike and the road from Bridport to Beaminster;

1764-5 Blandford and Poole Trust, established to extend the route from beyond Blandford via Bulbarrow to join the Sherborne Trust; it was later split into two divisions: a western division covering the roads west of Blandford (Vale of Blackmoor Trust); and an eastern division covering the roads south of Blandford (Blandford and Poole Trust);

1765-6 Blandford to Wimborne on the north side of the River Stour (Blandford & Wimborne Trust); Dorchester to Wareham, Corfe and Worth Matravers; Langton Matravers to East Lulworth; Wareham to Bere Regis (the last three administered by the Wareham Trust, the largest and most ambitious of the Dorset turnpike trusts);

1768-9 Wareham to Dorchester via Broadmayne (Dorchester & Wool Trust);

1769-70 Uplyme to Crewkerne (Lyme Regis & Crewkerne Trust);

1776-7 Frampton to Wyke Regis via Winterbourne Abbas, Portesham, Chickerell and Abbotsbury (Abbotsbury & Bridport Trust);

1777-8 Broadwindsor to Woolcombe via Beaminster and Evershot; Maiden Newton to South Perrot and Crewkerne (Maiden Newton Trust).

It is difficult to know whether the omission on the map of roads which had already been authorised before 1773 is an indication that they had not yet been turnpiked or that the map itself is not up-to-date. Nonetheless those that are shown are clearly delineated with bolder lines and Bayly's map is helpful for the road historian.

THOMAS CONDER, 1784

George Augustus Walpole (or Walpoole, as he is styled on his maps) was a topographer with only one work to his name, *The New British Traveller*, published by Alexander Hogg in 1784. He was assisted in the preparation of this five-part work by 'A Society of Gentlemen'. The atlas contains twenty-three maps of the English counties, often with two or more counties on the same page. All but one of the county plates (Berkshire and Somerset, by Thomas Bowen) were engraved by Thomas Conder.

The Dorset map, measuring 165 mm x 100 mm, is one of four counties to a page – Middlesex, Surrey, Dorset and Sussex. Dorset is the lower left-hand of the four, which adjoin one another with no space between the frames. It is pleasantly engraved, carefully coloured in pinks, yellows and greens, and the title cartouche consists of a picture of a block of Portland stone. The map is old-fashioned looking and is not at all up-to-date as far as turnpike roads are concerned, in spite of its claim that it is 'A New Map of DORSETSHIRE Drawn from the Latest Authorities'. This is a typically high-flown claim of the late eighteenth century, made in this case by a publisher who had not made any effort to include the latest information.

In the lower left-hand corner, the Arms of Dorchester are displayed on a badge-shaped shield. Sadly, with regard to the

Thomas Conder, 1784.

road system, the county town is not given its due status as the hub of the turnpike roads. This is surprising, since between 1750 and 1780 the turnpike roads in Dorset had trebled in number and yet this map does not make any attempt to include them. The turnpikes to Sherborne, Frampton (following the route on the north side of the Frome), Abbotsbury, Wareham and Salisbury (via Pimperne, Tarrant Hinton, Cashmoor and Woodyates) are all omitted. Compare it with the smaller map from *Cary's Traveller's Companion* in the next chapter, published only eight years later, and you will see the difference. Cary's map shows nearly all the turnpike roads.

The year in which Conder's map was published was a momentous one for road development: in August 1784 there was the first trial run of a mail coach service, from Bristol to London, initiated by Thomas Palmer of Bath. Carrying four inside passengers and an armed guard for the security of the mail, it covered the distance remarkably quickly, leaving Bath at 5.20 p.m. and reaching the GPO in Lombard Street at 8 o'clock the following morning. There was no doubt that this was both a speedy and a safe method of transporting the mail and the experiment was an immediate success.

By November 1785 a mail coach network had been established at Palmer's instigation throughout England, including the two routes through Dorset – to Exeter and to Poole. The impact of mail coaches on the road system was dramatic, because the coaches were directly responsible for the burgeoning of road improvements under Thomas Telford and John Loudon McAdam.

There was also a profound social effect, because the coaches carried news. Since they ran to a strict schedule, they could be counted on to arrive at the expected time. The townspeople waited eagerly for the latest tidings, shouted by the guard or, sometimes more reliably, posted on handbills.

There was one further edition of Walpole's atlas, ten years afterwards, in 1794, with the expanded title of *The New and Complete British Traveller*, again prepared by 'A Society of Gentlemen', but now 'revised, corrected and improved' by William Hugh Dalton. The maps in this edition were no different from their predecessors, and stood little chance in competition with John Cary's excellent productions for the traveller at around the same time.

Consistent with the old-fashioned look of Conder's map, there is an unusually late reference to Studland Castle, which does not normally appear on maps after about 1690. Note also the return to the wording 'British Channel', as used in Owen and Bowen's *Britannia Depicta* sixty-four years earlier, instead of the more usual 'English Channel' of this period. These and other features combine to give this map a feel of outmoded antiquity; hardly the thing for the 'new British traveller'!

It is remarkable that only three years after Conder's inadequate, backward-looking map for travellers appeared, *Cary's New and Correct English Atlas* was published, showing not only a really comprehensive road system, but also a style of cartography which would shape future map-making – a style which was adopted by the Ordnance Survey and which continued to be the standard for map-makers thereafter.

JOHN CARY, 1787

The main link between map-making in the eighteenth and nineteenth centuries was the cartographer, publisher and engraver John Cary. Newly established at the time of the great triumvirate, Thomas Kitchin, Thomas Bowen and Emanuel Bowen, he was so successful that he was commissioned by the

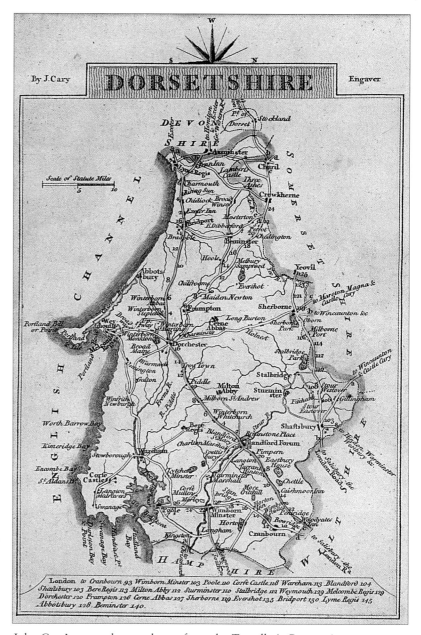

John Cary's unusual rotated map from the *Traveller's Companion*, 1792.

Postmaster-General to undertake a survey of all the main roads of the country. This led to *Cary's New Map of England and Wales, with Part of Scotland*, published in 1794, which showed a departure from mapping on a county basis, a practice that had been followed for over two hundred years, since Saxton and

Norden set the trend in Elizabethan times.

However, the maps most relevant to those of Dorset are from three important publications: *Cary's New and Correct English Atlas*, published in 1787; *Cary's Traveller's Companion*, published in 1790, containing miniature county maps, some of them dated 1789; and *Cary's New English Atlas*, published in 1809. Maps from these three publications, ranging from miniature (93 mm x 123 mm) to folio (480 mm x 530 mm) show the remarkable extent of John Cary's cartographical achievement. Each atlas became a popular publication in its own right and all were reprinted in many editions.

The example illustrated, measuring 93 mm x 123 mm, from the 1792 edition of his *Traveller's Companion*, breaks new ground in all sorts of different ways. It is unusual, in that Dorset has been rotated with west at the top and east at the lower end of the page, in order to make it fit into the pocket-size format of the atlas, although the place names are aligned horizontally in the usual way. Along the lower edge of the map there is a helpful list of 22 of the chief towns, showing their distances in statute miles from London.

Another innovation is the marking of the distances between towns at two-mile intervals instead of single distances in stages, thus favouring a system invented by John Ogilby rather than using another pioneered by Thomas Kitchin. The latter's device, however, is the one that has stuck and we now take it for granted that we will find distances in stages between towns (or other convenient points) marked on modern road maps.

The roads on this map are largely up-to-date and reflect Cary's high standards of map-making. Nearly all the latest turnpike roads are included (depicted with firm double-lines) and the two mail-coach routes are coloured green to emphasise their importance. However, the turnpike link from Beaminster through Evershot to Woolcombe is not shown, nor is the turnpike from Frampton to Wyke Regis through Winterbourne Abbas, Portesham and Chickerell. The turnpike from Wareham to Worth Matravers through Corfe is shown, although the turnpike from Swanage to Lulworth via Kingston, Steeple and Tyneham is not; nor is the continuation of the turnpike from the Horton Inn towards Shaftesbury.

Two non-turnpike roads are shown. The first is a loop running south from Shaftesbury to Sturminster Newton, through Stalbridge and back to Shaftesbury through Fifehead Magdalen. The last part of this loop is intriguing because it follows the path of the old West Road and indicates that the road from Fifehead Magdalen to Stour Provost, crossing the River Stour at Stour Provost Mill, was probably still in use in the late eighteenth century.

The other non-turnpike road is the branch from Blandford to Milton Abbey. The spelling of the latter word looks odd without the 'e', although this was a perfectly acceptable spelling, listed in Dr. Samuel Johnson's 1755 *Dictionary of the English Language*. However, to the right of the title-cartouche there is a genuine spelling error, where Cary (surprisingly for an engraver with his reputation for accuracy) misses out the first 'r' in the word 'engraver'.

He picks out a dozen country estates, eleven of which have been highlighted in green. Bubb Dodington's Eastbury House is marked, although it had been largely demolished by 1782. Close by stands Chettle House, the present house having been built by George Chafin in 1810. St. Giles's House near Wimborne St. Giles was the seat of the Earl of Shaftesbury. Also shown are Melbury Sampford (Earl of Ilchester), Sherborne Park (Lord Digby), Stalbridge Park (Earl of Uxbridge), Bryanstone Place (Lord Portman), Horton and More Crichel (Humphrey Sturt), Charborough Park near Sturminster Marshall (Thomas Erle Drax) and Came House, south of Dorchester (John Damer). The one not highlighted in green is Merley House, near Wimborne Minster, then belonging to Ralph Willett.

By the date of this map main roads were beginning to be properly metalled in order to cope with the vastly increased traffic. In the mid-eighteen hundreds the first sprung coaches were invented and their rapid development led to faster and more efficient travel. Coaching inns played an important part in the system, providing fresh horses for the next stage and accommodation for weary travellers. Cary was the first to mark these inns on his maps, such as the Woodyates Inn and Caishmoor Inn on the Salisbury to Blandford turnpike, and the Exeter Inn, Rising Sun and Penn Inn on the Bridport to Axminster turnpike. The Horton Inn, still in use today at a busy country cross-roads, is marked as being on a T-junction, although by the time this map was made the turnpike continued as far as the Great Western Turnpike between Thickthorn and Cashmoor.

This is the first map to show the new section of road from Wimborne to Cranborne on the east of the River Allen, instead of the old road on the west side, which used to cross the river at Little Hinton (see page 34).

A final point of note is that Cary was the first to use the Meridian of Greenwich on British maps, although it was not until 1884 that the Meridian was established as nought degrees Longitude by international agreement. Cary's innovative use of the Meridian, combined with the accuracy and clarity of his maps, and the modern style of his work, puts him in the top rank of British cartographers.

John Aiken, 1790. A simple map for the classroom

JOHN AIKEN, 1790

This simple map of Dorset, by John Aiken, cartographer and man of letters, was published in 1790, in the second edition of *England Delineated* (the first edition had no maps). Subsequent editions, except for the last one published in 1818, contained forty-three simplistic maps intended for school children, giving no other detail than the towns and rivers of the forty English counties, and of England and North and South Wales.

Measuring 160 mm x 100 mm, the map has a striking dearth of information, and, with no continuation of the coastline to east and west, the county floats like an island on the creamy background. Because of the lack of boundary markings, a stretch of water that is not particularly visible on Speed's map 180 years earlier is thrown into relief, namely Luckford Lake, shown flowing into the Frome. However, the engraver has mistaken its true source at Povington Barrow near Tyneham and has linked it with the coast, thereby giving 'Purbeck Isle' a truly insular appearance.

As on earlier maps where the information is sparse, it is interesting to note what the map-maker has decided to include. Apart from the larger towns that one would expect to see marked, the other place names have either ecclesiastical or royal significance. Abbotsbury, Cerne Abbas, Milton Abbas and Cranborne each had an abbey or a priory, and Bere Regis was kept for a time by King John, who had a residence there. Bere

Regis's status was further enhanced in the reign of Henry VII, when Dorset-born Cardinal Morton, whose ancestors on his mother's side (the Turbervilles) were interred in the church, rebuilt and embellished this edifice, the magnificent timber roof being his great memorial.

The importance of these places waned as time went by, but not to the extent that they were completely bypassed, since all but one of these (Milton Abbas) was eventually served by a turnpike road. In the 1860s the abolition of the turnpikes was agreed and after 1888 all main roads became the responsibility of the new county councils. Out-of-the-way places thus became backwaters and their demise was complete, unless they were served by a railway. Of the five places mentioned, only Abbotsbury was reached by a branch line (from Upwey Junction, opened in 1885), so its contact with the outside world was temporarily extended until the line's closure in 1952.

On most counties in this series, the title appears at the top of the map. Dorset is one of the exceptions. The book, when published, was popular, running into many editions. There was a third in 1795, and others in 1800, 1803 and 1809. This example is from the 1800 edition. The simplicity of the maps has given them a unique charm, much appreciated by collectors, and their popularity remains undiminished.

TOWN PLANS, 1774 & 1799

Many plans of Dorset towns are available and a good source is Hutchins' *History of Dorset*. The *History* contains plans of Bridport, Dorchester, Poole, Shaftesbury (1615 & 1799), Wareham, Wimborne Minster and Weymouth (1774, an updated version of the 1774 plan & a plan from circa 1804).

I have selected plans from four corners of the county: Poole, Bridport, Weymouth and Shaftesbury.

The Poole plan (which is in all three editions of Hutchins' *History*, but dates from the 1774 first edition) is wonderfully detailed. The inscription reads: 'To Coll: [Colonel] Thomas Calcraft and Joshua Mauger Esq.rs This PLAN of POOLE engrav'd at their expence is inscribed by their humble Servant The AUTHOR'. It is surmounted by The Arms of Poole.

On the facing page there is 'A Prospect of the Town of POOLE from the West End of BRUNCKSEY ISLAND', engraved by J. Mynde and drawn by John Bastard, who, with his brother William, was largely responsible for the redesigning and rebuilding of Blandford Forum after the disastrous fire of 1731.

Hutchins describes Poole as lying 'on the border of a barren, dreary heath, which affords no pleasant view to travellers who come from the more delightful parts of the county', but in reality late eighteenth century Poole was a bustling and prosperous port.

The Newfoundland fishing industry was a major factor in the town's flourishing fortunes. At the end of the War of the Spanish Succession the Treaty of Utrecht (1713) confirmed that Newfoundland was British territory. After years of conflict with France over possession of this lucrative fishing-ground, the merchants involved in the Newfoundland trade were able to develop the massive cod-fisheries and brought unprecedented prosperity, not only to the Borough of Poole but also to the surrounding area.

A spate of fine building took place and Poole is now endowed with a heritage of Georgian architecture (civic, domestic and ecclesiastical) which stands as a permanent memorial to its splendid past.

The plan of Bridport (also in all three editions of Hutchins), is, by contrast with Poole, that of a small market town and the

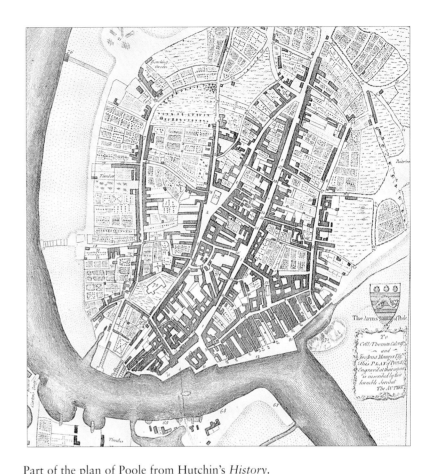

Part of the plan of Poole from Hutchin's *History*.
1. High-street. 2. Market-street. 3. Pillory-street. 4. Hill-street. 5. Church-street. 6. Quay-street. 7. West-street. 8. Langland-street. 9. Strand-street. 10. Great-quay. 11. Little-quay. 12. New-quay. 13. Paradise-street. 14. Salisbury-street. 15. Hancock-alley. 16. Thomas-alley. 17. Barber's-lane. 18. Bay-hog-lane. 19. Fowler's-lane. 20. West-butt-street. 21. West-butt-green. 22. West-butt-lane. 23. Market-lane. 24. Lover's-lane. 25. Hunger-hill. 26. Nightingale-lane. 27. Town-gates-lane. 28. Crooked-lane. 29. Short-way. 30. Water-lane. 31. Pound-lane. 32. Deerhay-lane. 33. Carter's-lane. 34. Fricker's-alley. 35. New Orchard. 36. New-street. 37. Cinnamon-lane. 38. Quay-lane. 39. Ditch-lane. 40. Bennet's-alley. 41. Crabb-lane. 42. Roger's lane. 43. Rozer's-lane. 44. Mud-lane. 45. Button's-lane. 46. Pluddie-lane. 47. Smock-alley. 48. Pelley's-lane. 49. Petty-lane. 50. Sutton's-piles. 51. Little-lane. 52. Toop's-lane. 53. Bell-lane. 54. Fish-street. 55. Skinner's-alley. 56. Old Orchard. 57. Weston's-lane. 58. Compton's-alley. 59. Levet's-lane. 60. Great Mount-lane. 61. Little-Mount-lane. 62. Green-lane. 63. Baiter-lane. 64. Hiley's-lane. 65. Drake's-alley. 66. Love-lane. 67. Perry-garden. 68. Ham-quays. 69. Ham-street. 70. Horse-island. 71. Oyster-bank. 72. Church. 73. Market-house. 74. Rope-walks. 75. Ham-street. 76. Bathing-house. 77. Baptist Meeting-house. 78. Great Meeting-house. 79. Small Meeting-house. 80. Quaker's Meeting. 81. Fish-shambles.

legend contains just six locations (five of which are of religious significance). The inscription reads: 'To Rich.d Brodrepp of Mapperton Esq.r Recorder of this Borough this PLAN, is most Respectfully inscrib'd by The Author'. It is surmounted by the Bridport Arms.

The watery location of Bridport is emphasised by the stream which surrounds it on three points of the compass. These orientations give their names to the three main streets: West Street, East Street and South Street. Eight other streets are named: Weeks Court Lane, Downe Street, Stake Lane, St. Michaels Lane, Gundrey Lane, Folly Mill Lane, Church Lane and Irish Lane. Three mills are mentioned: West Mill, South Mill and Folly Mill. Perhaps the most attractive feature of this plan is the south-east view of St. Mary's Church, engraved by John Bayly, who also engraved the frontispiece map in Hutchins' first edition of the *History of Dorset*.

'The Plan of the Town of WEYMOUTH and MELCOMBE REGIS' has the heavy look of an eighteenth century print and is an updated version of the same map in Hutchins' first edition of 1774, showing the newly constructed sea-wall along the 'Back Water'. The five horse-drawn bathing machines serve to remind us that Weymouth was a favoured resort of George III from 1789 onwards.

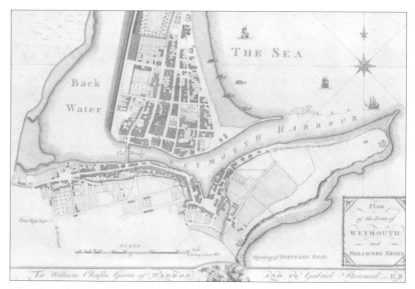

The plan of Weymouth. Note the five bathing machines

The Shaftesbury plan, dated 1799, is found only in the rare second edition of Hutchins' *History*. It was published according to Act of Parliament, October 20th, 1799 by W. Upjohn, Land Surveyor. Engraved by T. I. Woodman, it is remarkable for its clarity, accuracy and its extraordinary range of copperplate script, the many styles of which are apparent in the dedication cartouche: 'TO THE Right Honourable ANTHONY ASHLEY COOPER Earl of Shaftesbury; Baron Ashley of Winborne St. Giles', Baron Cooper of Powlett in the County of Somerset; Lord of the Manor of SHAFTESBURY, and Patron of the Churches there, this PLAN of the TOWN, is by Permission humbly dedicated by His obedient Servant W.m Upjohn.'

A history of the town is detailed on either side of the coat-of-arms below the plan, including a pleasant description: 'Shaftesbury is delightfully situated on a high Hill, in the Northern Part of Dorsetshire, on the great Road from London to Cornwall. The Air is pure & very salubrious but the high situation of the Town makes it rather cold. A weekly Market is held here on Saturday, which is well frequented, and thought to be the best in the West of England for Butter.' The Butter Cross in the Commons was removed in 1727, probably to create more road space for the coaches and wagons which were gradually replacing the movement of men and pack animals.

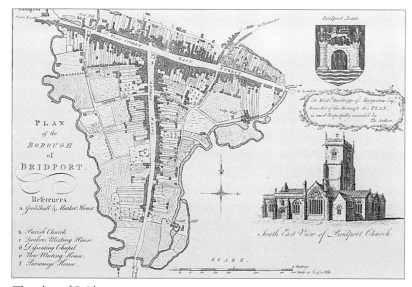

The plan of Bridport.

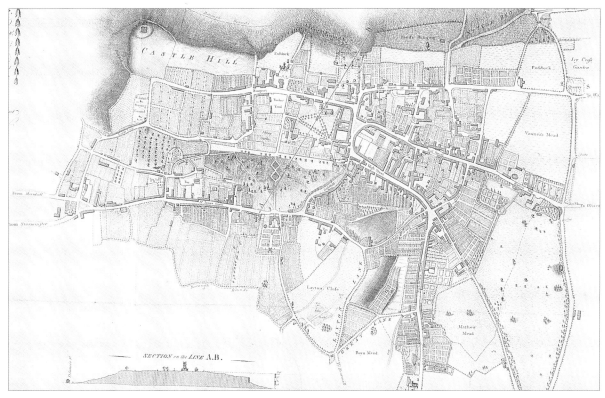

The plan of Shaftesbury. The detail on Upjohn's plan is exceptional, down to trees and paths.

The stage coaches which operated from soon after the mid-seventeenth century were little faster than the stage wagons that lumbered from place to place, carrying goods as well as people, so the mail continued to be carried by post boys on horse back for another hundred years. Because of its situation on the West Road, Shaftesbury had early prominence in the post office organisation initiated by Cromwell. Appointed in 1667, the town's first post master, Captain Fry, lived at the Angel Inn on the site of the present Post Office. Dorchester did not have a Post Office for another 30 years.

William Upjohn was born in Shaftesbury in 1770 and he knew the town intimately. His plan is so detailed that individual trees can de distinguished. He shows the elegant gardens of the larger Georgian houses and the vegetable plots of the others. Only one house is actually named – that of the 'late Sir T. Arundell' (K). The double-lozenge path leading down from Abbey Walk remains unchanged today, though there is no longer the formal walled garden at its end, there being instead the informal garden of The Two Brewers public house. Although St. Peter's (A) is shown in plan, the medieval Holy Trinity (B) is accurately drawn in perspective. Three Non-conformist meeting houses are defined: the Quakers' in St. James's Street (E), the Presbyterians' in Mustons Lane (F) and the Methodists' in Bell Street (G). The old Guild Hall is marked (H) and the Sessions Hall at the back of the Red Lion (I).

It is interesting to note that a few of the street names are slightly different: Copper Street (now Coppice Street), Blyke Street or Ram Street (now Bleke Street) and Muttons Lane (now Mustons Lane). The rest are the same today, including Gold Hill, which may have been named (like Copper Street) after the coins minted in the town prior to the Norman Conquest. It is named Gould Hill on the 1615 plan of Shaftesbury in Hutchins' *History*, reflecting the contemporary pronunciation. Upjohn's original copper plate can be viewed at Shaftesbury Museum.

The Nineteenth Century

THE ORDNANCE SURVEY, 1801 (1811)

The realisation that an accurate map and good roads are essential to maintain military dominance was driven home to the government of George II during the Jacobite Rebellion. Following the 1715 Jacobite uprising, General George Wade was ordered to open up the Highlands by building military roads designed for the rapid deployment of troops to crush any further rebellion. More than 230 miles of road and 30 bridges were constructed and a number of maps were made. The same roads were used by the Young Pretender, Charles Edward Stuart ('Bonnie Prince Charlie'), who rode as far south as Derby before his army was finally defeated at Culloden in 1746 by William Augustus, Duke of Cumberland (the second son of George II). The Duke's officers found themselves 'embarrassed for want of a proper survey of the country.' On his return to London the Duke received royal consent from his father for the mapping of Scotland and thus the first comprehensive large-scale national survey of any country in the British Isles was set in motion.

The Military Survey of Scotland (or 'Roy's Map') was undertaken between 1747 and 1755 by William Roy, 'Surveyor-General of Coasts and Engineer for making Surveys under the Honourable Board of Ordnance'. This remarkably talented man had the foresight to realise that a full and accurate large-scale survey of Great Britain was an absolute necessity, but his efforts were frustrated first by the Seven Years War (1756–1763) and then by the American War of Independence (1775–1783).

Roy had realised from early on that the only effective implementation of the survey could be in peacetime. A surveying party consisted of a surveyor, one non-commissioned officer and six soldiers: 'One carried the Instrument (a theodolite); two

measured with the Chain; two for the Fore and Back Stations; and one as Batman.' At the outbreak of war officers and soldiers were withdrawn from the task for active service, so the national survey went into abeyance for a number of years. The scheme might have foundered altogether, but for the intervention of a long-time supporter of Roy, the Duke of Richmond, who persuaded the government to give its support. At last, in 1791 (the year after Roy's death), the Trigonometrical Survey of the Board of Ordnance was established in the Tower of London and Colonel William Mudge became its director.

The first county to be surveyed was Kent, drawn by William Faden for the Board of Ordnance and published in January 1801. The other southern counties followed, Dorset being mapped ten years later in 1811. By the year 1844, surveys had been completed as far north as Hull. Much of the later success of what was to become the Ordnance Survey was due to General Colby, who established the 13th Survey Company, Royal Engineers, in 1824.

The example illustrated is from folding O.S. sheet number XVI (measuring 790 mm x 620 mm opened out), which shows the stretch of coastline from Worbarrow Bay to the mouth of the Bourne River (what is now the centre of Bournemouth), on a scale of one inch to one mile, the chosen scale of the Ordnance Survey. The map was engraved on copper plates and displays the finest qualities of the engraver's art. Accuracy was paramount and the detail is phenomenal.

The more detailed illustration, on page 70, shows Poole Harbour, as well as Wareham and Poole. The detail is exceptional, with the individual streets and buildings in the two towns clearly visible. Around Poole one's attention is drawn to

The section covering Worbarrow Bay to what is now Bournemouth from the first Ordnance Survey map of Dorset, 1811.

the local industry with many references to 'Brick Kilns', 'Clay Houses' and 'Iron Mills'. On the Wareham panel the 'Iron Railway' linking the Wareham to Corfe Castle road with Middlebeere Quay for the transport of clay is so detailed that you can see the cutting and passing places. The channels in Poole Harbour are clearly defined and although buoys have replaced the stakes marking the main channel, and the arrival of the cross-Channel ferry service has led to an immense amount of dredging, all the smaller channels follow much the same course as today.

This map consists of eighteen panels on linen, with marbled endpapers, designed to fold into a neat 160 mm x 250 mm pocket-sized map, foreshadowing the modern folding OS maps so familiar to us today. The imprint on the lower margin states 'Published 10th April 1811 by Lt. Col. Mudge, Tower, Engraved at the Drawing Room in the Tower. By Benjn. Baker and Assistants – The Writing by Ebenr. Bourne.' The imprint on the top left margin states simply: 'Price Three Shillings.' There is a tiny rectangle of paper pasted to the cover, showing a simple outline of the coastline, the overlap from the adjoining map and the figure 16. This ready reference, avoiding the need to unfold the map to discover the area depicted, is another tradition that has carried through to the modern OS maps.

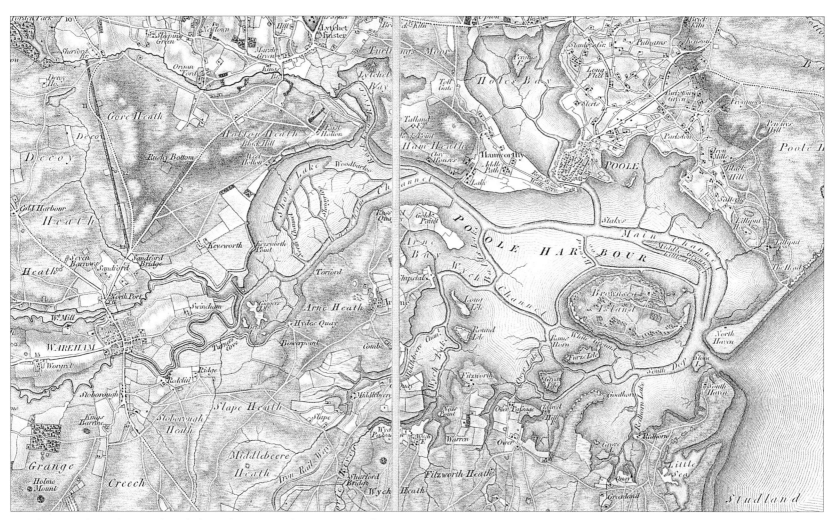

Wareham, Poole Harbour and Poole from the 1811 Ordnance Survey of Dorset.

JAMES BAKER, 1802

Reminiscent of George Bickham's bird's-eye view of 1750, James Baker's novel concept of depicting a route with a sequence of miniature scenes appeared in *The Imperial Guide*, sold by Symonds in 1802 (see page 72). Measuring 105 mm x 180 mm, the illustration is part of the mail-coach road from London to Weymouth, entering the picture near Andover. Each thumbnail sketch is named in the margin with its mileage from London.

We pick up the Dorset section at 'Woodyate Inn', 91 miles from the capital. The next location is 'Hanly' (Sixpenny Handley), followed by 'Cashmore' (Cashmoor), 'Hinton' (Tarrant Hinton), 'Pimperne', 'Highcamp' (now Blandford Army Camp), 'Blandford', 'Brianstone House' (formerly Lord Portman's residence), 'Whitchurch' (Winterborne Whitechurch), 'Milbourn' (Milborne St. Andrew), 'Dewlish', 'Piddletown' (Puddletown), 'Cunningham', 'Kingston House' (Kingston Maurward), 'Dorchester', 'Herringstone' (Winterborne Herringston), 'Maiden Castle and Ridgeway Hill', 'Upway' (Upwey) and, finally, with its inviting seaside view, 'Weymouth', 127 miles away from London.

In July 1802 Colonel Robert Browne travelled this route to dine in Upwey with his brother-in-law, Richard Steward, who was standing for Parliament in the election in Weymouth. Over a three-day period, the colonel records his movements and costs in his daily journal. On the first day, Wednesday 7th, he set off in a gig from Aylesbury at 11.30 a.m., had tea in Newbury for one and sixpence, supped in Andover for 3 shillings and travelled all night. On the second day, after breakfast in Dorchester, he arrived in Weymouth at 10.30 a.m. and dined and slept at Mr Steward's in Upwey.

This meticulous army officer's notes record the travelling costs: the chaise, driver and turnpike from Andover to Salisbury cost £1. 2s. 6d; from Salisbury to Woodyates Inn cost 14 shillings; from Woodyates to Blandford 15 shillings; Blandford to Dorchester 19 shillings and sixpence; and Dorchester to Weymouth (including breakfast in Dorchester) 14 shillings. Colonel Browne's entire journey from Aylesbury to Weymouth, including meals and paying Mr Steward's servants, cost £10. 1s. 10d., a hugely expensive undertaking by today's standards.

The third day's entry in the journal records the election results: 'Mr Steward 126, Sir J Pultney 107, Mr Garthshore 100, Mr Adam 99, Mr Arbuthnot 74'; so his brother-in-law won the election and (no doubt after some celebration at the weekend) on Monday 12th July, 1802, he returned, taking the Royal Mail from Dorchester at 5 p.m., supped and slept at the White Hart in Andover, set off early the following morning at 5.30 a.m. and was back in Aylesbury on Tuesday 13th by 4 p.m. This unique record gives an insight into the nature of travelling in the early nineteenth century.

On his return journey from Weymouth, it should still have been light enough for Colonel Browne to glimpse Blandford parish church, whose distinctive tower is clearly visible above the rooftops in Baker's drawing. Blandford, having been partly burned down in 1713 and then almost completely destroyed by a disastrous fire in 1731, was rebuilt during a period of intense activity between the date of the second fire and 1766. Chief amongst the new monuments was the parish church of St. Peter and St. Paul, designed by master-builders John and William Bastard and finished in 1739.

Other important new buildings included the Town Hall and Coupar House. Because of the integral nature of the restoration, which was largely guided by the Bastard brothers, Blandford Forum presents a remarkably entire picture of an eighteenth-century market town.

Nearby 'Brianstone House' is depicted with a view of the James Wyatt building that replaced an earlier house demolished in 1778. Wyatt's house was in turn pulled down in 1890 and replaced by the present mansion, designed in the grand classical manner by Richard Norman Shaw. One of the largest English country houses to be built in modern times, it is currently home to Bryanston School.

Dewlish House was constructed by Thomas Skinner in 1702 and is a good example of domestic building of the period, containing high-quality eighteenth-century fittings. Kingston House (Kingston Maurward) was built of brick between 1717 and 1720 for George Pitt of Stratfield Say. Important alterations were made in 1794 when the exterior was cased in Portland stone and the mansion became the dignified classical composition we see today.

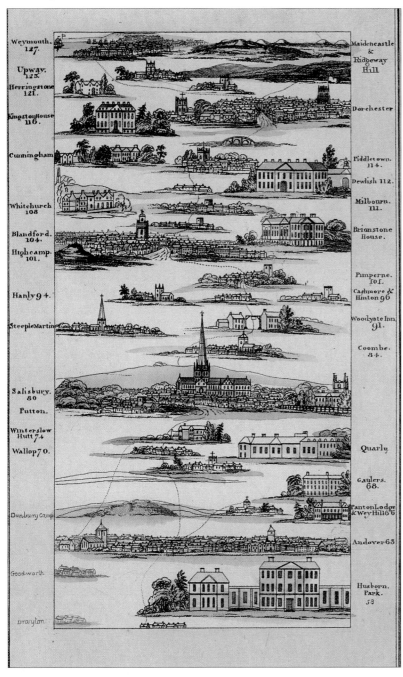

James Baker, 1802. Baker's imaginative use of perspective drawing brings to life the topography of the route to Weymouth. It is quite possible that George III would have consulted this 'map' on his way to the resort.

The owner at the time of this map was William Morton Pitt, grandson of George Pitt.

This unusual 'map' is fascinating for its detail and for its charming hand-coloured sketches. The whole page is no more than a series of tiny perspective drawings with the prominent feature in each case being the major place of worship, echoing the custom on antique maps of locating towns and cities with the conventional sign (often coloured red) of a church, abbey, minster or cathedral, smaller or larger according to status and population. Here Salisbury Cathedral takes pride of place, the height of its spire accentuated by means of the drawing overlapping some of the scenes above.

JOHN LUFFMAN, 1803

This tiny circular map, measuring 60 mm in diameter, offers scant geographical information, possibly the least of any map of Dorset ever produced. Its cameo view of the county is as if seen through a spyglass. The border informs the reader of the county depicted, the number of members (20) it sends to Parliament, the scale of 20 miles and that Dorchester is the county town, 120 miles from London.

The main roads through the county are simply and clearly drawn, with the names of towns en route. The absence of cross-roads and villages emphasises the simplicity and clarity of the map, whilst the thumbnail description below it gives some basic information about the county – two years after the first official census in 1801.

A New Pocket Atlas and Geography of England and Wales was published by John Luffman in 1803 and contained fifty-four miniature plates plus an index map of England. Although the maps are of comparatively recent origin, they are extremely scarce, because the mortality rate for smaller maps is higher than for larger ones. The atlas may have been used for teaching geography in Georgian times, so there may yet be copies lurking unnoticed in households.

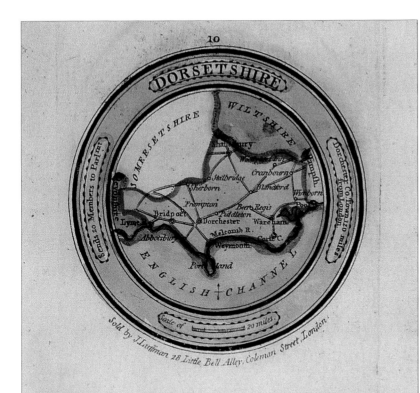

DORSETSHIRE is upwards of 50 miles in length from east to west, and near 40 in breadth from north to south. It is divided into 34 hundreds, which contain 22 market towns, 248 parishes, and 22,262 houses. The population amounts to 115,319.

This county enjoys a mild and wholesome air, and a rich and fertile soil, except on the side of Hampshire towards the sea; and as far as Blandford it is one extensive heath. Dorset is famous for its woollen manufactures and fine beer. Its other productions are corn, cattle, and hemp, Portland and Purbeck stones, and pipe clay. The principal rivers are the Stour and the Frome.

John Luffman, 1803.

ENCLOSURE MAP, 1810

Enclosure of common land had been happening for centuries, not always with the approval of those concerned, witness the riots which followed the disafforestation of Gillingham Forest in 1624. Enclosure attempted to rationalise the use of land by means of allotments and very often it was the lowly user of common grazing land who lost out to the new landowners. It is true that many of the earlier enclosures were carried out by agreement of the landlord and tenant without the expense of an Act of Parliament, but during the eighteenth century, small farms were being progressively squeezed out by the effects of new agricultural technology, much to the distress of the tenants.

Frequently landlords deliberately failed to renew tenures, adding the small tenements to the larger farms. The landlords could afford to pay for Acts of Parliament to be passed and these required the appointment of commissioners to supervise accurate surveys and, in theory, to ensure impartiality. In practice, the small farmers became common labourers, working long hours, poorly paid and inadequately housed. Their lot worsened during the Napoleonic Wars when the rising prices of farm produce ensured that if enclosure had not already happened it was almost bound to take place. Between 1793 and 1815 the price of beef, mutton and barley doubled, and the price of wheat trebled.

It is in this context that an Act of Parliament was passed for the Walditch Inclosure Commissioners Award, surveyed by William Summers in 1810 during the reign of George III. Measuring 510 mm x 465 mm, on a scale of 4 chains to the inch, it is a fold-out frontispiece map in a large, leather-bound, 18-page, handwritten award. The Commissioner was Alexander Law, who writes under oath before Thomas Abraham in the Golden Lion Inn in Bridport that he will 'execute and perform the several Trusts, Powers and Authorities' vested in him as a Commissioner 'by virtue of an Act for Inclosing Lands in the Parish of Walditch in the County of Dorset according to equity and good conscience and without favor [sic] or affection, prejudice or partiality.'

In a sense this is two maps in one, because it shows the three open fields in the parish that were in existence before the enclosure. Named Lower Field, Higher Field and East Field, they would have consisted of an inconvenient scattering of strips on common land available to the members of the parish by mutual agreement of use and tenure. As well as meadow and pasture, there would undoubtedly have been crops of hemp and flax, in view of the parish's proximity to Bridport.

The date of this enclosure comes not long after the Bounty Awards offered by Act of Parliament between 1782 and 1793 to all hemp and flax growers to help counteract the growing competition from abroad (by the late eighteenth century 75% of all hemp was imported from Russia). The Bounty Act promised to pay threepence (just over 1p) per stone (nearly 6½ kilos) for hemp and fourpence per stone for flax. To give some idea of the income that might be expected, an average crop produced 20-30 stones of fibre per acre.

After enclosure all three open fields were subdivided into allotments whose occupiers are listed in the award. The final page sets out 'The Rate for the Repairs of the Private Roads' (the Rates were calculated to add up to exactly £100, hence the odd amounts quoted below). The 'Proprietor in Possession' with the largest share of the enclosure was James Balston with two allotments, one in Lower Field and the other in Higher Field, totalling over 47 acres.

Balston also had to pay the highest 'Proportion of Rate': £19. 8s. 7 1/4 d. (almost 20% of the total Rate of £100). Next came William Draper Best with allotments of nearly twenty-six acres (his Rate is £16. 19s. 10 1/4 d.). At the bottom of the list there were the 'Walditch Churchwardens and Overseers of the Poor of the Parish' who got a triangle of land of a little over an acre and they were rated at four shillings and eleven pence three-farthings.

An important general point to note is that care for the poor and needy is embedded in English Law and that communal responsibility is part of the fabric of our society. The implications of this run deep and this important social thread remains constant through the ages, in spite of many alterations in the Law right up to the present day (see page 90).

An interesting aspect of enclosure is the rights of access to roads and footpaths. The 'Publick Footways' (Bradpole Footway, Loders Footway, Lums Footway and Shipton

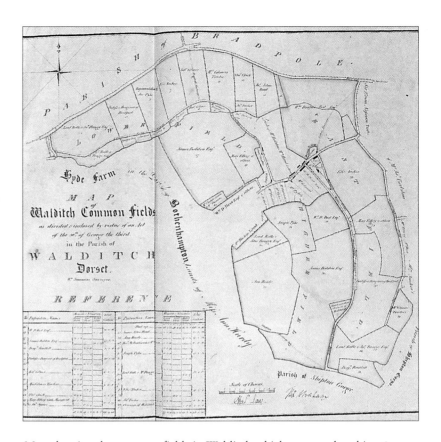

Map showing the common fields in Walditch which were enclosed in 1810.

Footway) are listed in the award, to establish that public right of access will continue. The award takes huge pains to ensure that the former 'Private Roads' will henceforth also have proper public access, 'either on foot or on horseback or with horses cattle waggons carts and carriages either loaded or unloaded or otherwise howsoever . . . of their free will and pleasure'. The 'Private Roads' in question were Lower Field Road, Puddicombes Road, Eastfield Road, Dunsfords Road, Tuckers Road and Higher Field Road.

The Summary of Enclosure lists the new proprietors' names and shows, amongst others, that three parcels of land were henceforth owned by the 'Bailiffs and Burgesses of Bridport'; another now belonged to the 'Rev.d Mr. Puddicombe and Mrs Warren' (the curate no doubt living in the eponymous road); and the largest number (four parcels) were the property of 'Lord Rolle and Mr Bragge'.

ROBERT ROWE, 1813

Hutchins' rare second edition of the *History of Dorset* has as its frontispiece 'A New Map of the County of Dorset Divided into Hundreds by R. Rowe, Jan. 1st 1813.' It was published at an epoch-making moment in the history of roads. Around 1811 John Loudon McAdam developed his 'macadamised system' of road construction, which was to supersede the metalled roads pioneered by John Metcalf in the second half of the eighteenth century. McAdam's cambered surface, made of tightly-packed crushed stone, was watertight and smooth, perfect for fast-moving coaches carrying passengers, luggage and mail. As speed increased, the division between traffic moving in opposite directions became an ever more important safety factor. Today we are used to road markings designed for this purpose and it is intriguing that the dotted lines along the middle of the Mail Coach Roads on the map bear an unmistakable likeness to the broken white lines running down the middle of modern roads.

A fascinating aspect of this is the question of why we drive on the left. Has this always been so? An excavation of a Roman quarry near Swindon has revealed that wagons drove on the left, because those leaving the quarry fully-laden made deeper ruts

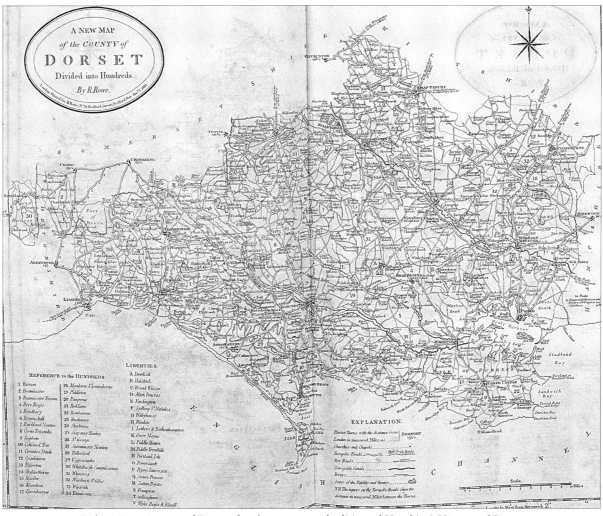

Robert Rowe's map of Dorset for the rare second edition of Hutchins' *History of Dorset*.

than the empty ones coming back. From medieval times the custom of driving on the left persisted, because carriage drivers liked to sit on the right to give their whip hands more freedom, and we still talk of someone in control as 'having the whip hand'. On the Continent, however, carriages were steered by a postillion, who sat on the left rear horse to gauge clearance between oncoming traffic.

On this map a new order of accuracy in road-measurement appears with distances from London to the main towns being marked to the nearest quarter of a mile. Relief is shown with shading which is sufficiently clear to allow the map-reader to imagine the ups and downs of the roads. A particularly interesting feature is the marking of the Dorset and Somerset Canal, which was never built, although an Act was passed in 1796 allowing the canal company to raise capital and buy land. By this time the canal boom was collapsing and the capital sums required were never realised. The canal would have run from the Kennet and Avon near Bradford to the Stour just below Shillingstone, from which point the river could have been made passable for barges to its mouth at Christchurch.

This is the first map in the book to mention Liberties. These were districts which were separate from the system of hundreds and were exempt from the jurisdiction of a sheriff. In other words, they ran their own affairs and were in effect a privately-owned hundred. In some cases, these were long-established, dating back many centuries. A liberty might once have been an 'honour', owned by a lord and recognised as having independent status owing to royal connection. Alternatively, if land was owned by an Oxford or Cambridge college, or by a college such as Eton or Winchester, it was recognised that jurisdiction lay with the owner and not with the authority locally. An example is Stour Provost, which was largely owned by King's College, Cambridge and was called Stour Provost, in deference to the title holder, the Provost of King's.

The same map appears in Robert Rowe's *The English Atlas*, published in 1816 and re-issued in 1829 as Henry Teesdale's *The New British Atlas*. Although Hutchins' 1861 third edition of the *History* states, as in the other two editions, that it is 'Adorned with a Correct Map of the County', in fact none was ever published.

The second edition of Hutchins' *History* met a most unfortunate fate. In 1808 there was a fire in the warehouse where the books were stacked awaiting distribution. All the unsold copies of the first and second volumes and the entire printed stock of the third volume (with the exception of one copy) were burnt. The original number of copies was never matched and their excellent plates were, over the years, broken up for sale individually, hence the rarity of the edition.

In 1792 Hutchins' son-in-law, Major Bellasis (who undertook the enlarged second edition with the help of a team of antiquaries and rose to the rank of Major-General in the East India Company), erected an oval plaque to his father-in-law's memory. The simple memorial is high up on the south wall of St. Edward's Chapel, the oldest part of Lady St. Mary Church in Wareham.

EDWARD LANGLEY AND WILLIAM BELCH, 1817

Edward Langley was the senior partner in the well-established London printing and publishing firm of Langley and Belch. He collaborated with William Belch early in his career and the two names were regarded as synonymous until 1820, when the partnership broke up. In 1818, two years before this parting of the ways, the firm produced a very attractive atlas called *Langley's New County Atlas of England and Wales*. The fifty-two maps were dated variously between 1816 and 1818 and each had a vignette of a town view or a building contained within the county. Every map in the series was headed 'Langley's new Map of . . . [name of county].'

The Dorset example, measuring 254 mm x 171 mm and dated 1817, has an unusual view of Weymouth from the east end of the town, with Portland visible in the background. Fishermen and their boats fill the foreground, and the view is captioned 'Esplanade Weymouth'.

Down the right-hand side the Hundreds and Liberties are listed. Each town on the map is marked with its distance from London. Minor roads are signified with narrow lines, turnpikes with broader lines and the Great Western Turnpike forges its way boldly through the centre of the map, coloured brown with

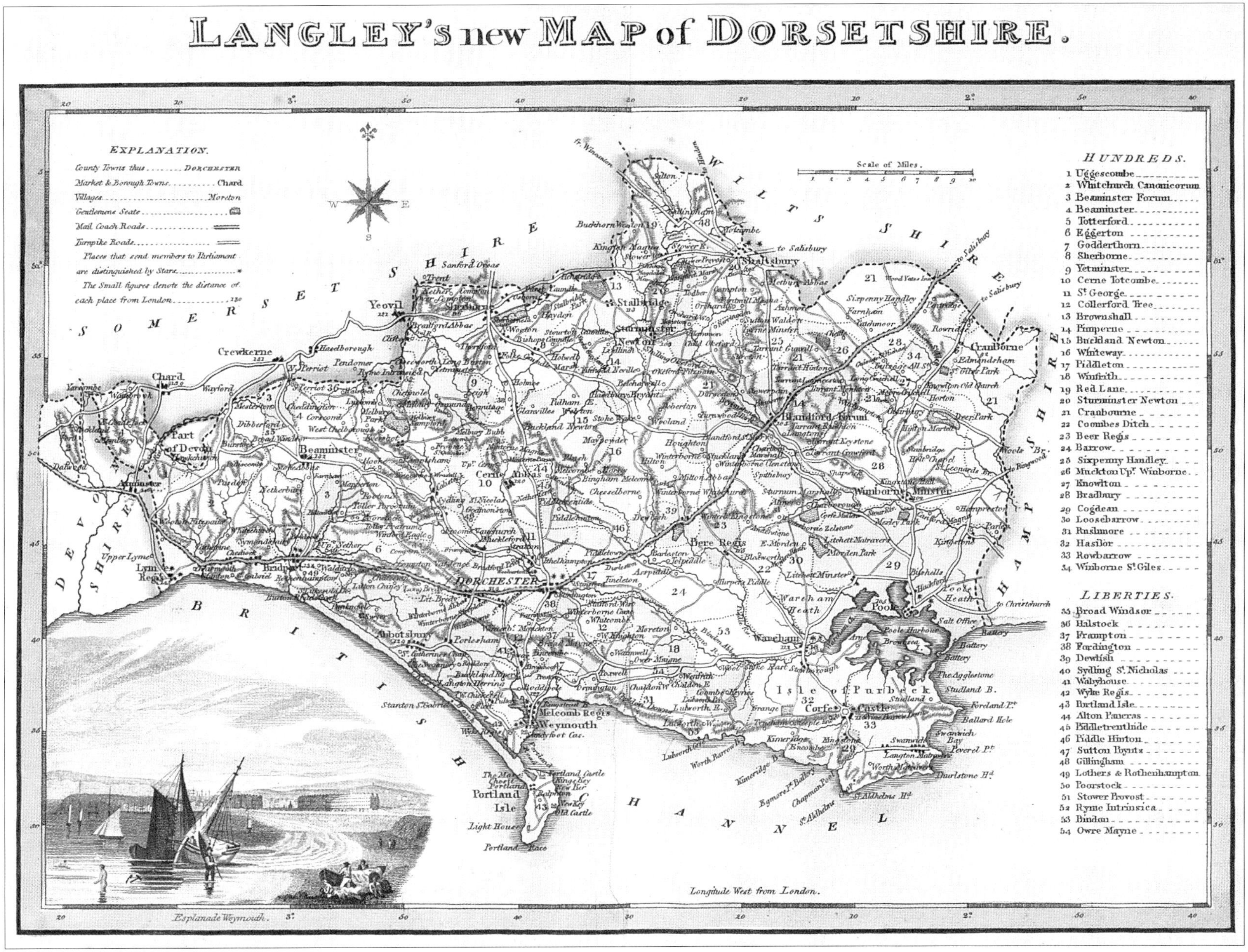

LANGLEY's new MAP of DORSETSHIRE.

Scale of Miles.

HUNDREDS.

1 Uggescombe
2 Whitchurch Canonicorum
3 Beaminster Forum
4 Beaminster
5 Totterford
6 Eggerton
7 Godderthorn
8 Sherborne
9 Yetminster
10 Cerne Totcombe
11 St George
12 Collerford Tree
13 Brownshall
14 Pimperne
15 Buckland Newton
16 Whiteway
17 Piddleton
18 Winfrith
19 Red Lane
20 Sturminster Newton
21 Cranbourne
22 Coombes Ditch
23 Beer Regis
24 Barrow
25 Sixpenny Handley
26 Muckton Up. Winborne
27 Knowlton
28 Bradbury
29 Cogdean
30 Loosebarrow
31 Rushmore
32 Haslor
33 Rowbarrow
34 Winborne St Giles

LIBERTIES.

35 Broad Windsor
36 Halstock
37 Frampton
38 Fordington
39 Dewlish
40 Sydling St Nicholas
41 Wabyhouse
42 Wyke Regis
43 Portland Isle
44 Alton Pancras
45 Piddletrenthide
46 Piddle Hinton
47 Sutton Poyntz
48 Gillingham
49 Lothers & Rothenhampton
50 Poorstock
51 Stower Provost
52 Ryme Intrinsica
53 Bindon
54 Owre Mayne

Longitude West from London.

Esplanade Weymouth.

Dorset, from *Langley's New County Atlas of England and Wales,* 1817. The series was the last to carry decorative features done in copper-plate engraving.

serrations along its edges for emphasis. It is odd that the two other mail coach roads (the West Road and the Ringwood to Poole road) are not given due prominence, since they were thriving routes at this time.

Various 'Gentlemens Seats' are depicted as enclosures with palings, namely Melbury Park, Sherborne Park, Stalbridge Park, Bryanston Park, Chettle, St. Giles Park, Moore Critchell Park, Horton Deer Park, Merley Park, Charborough Park, Morden Park, Milborne St. Andrew, Grange and Lulworth Park. What we know as Kingston Lacy is marked Kingstone Hall. The largely demolished Eastbury House no longer gets a mention.

The seat at Milborne St. Andrew is rarely shown on maps because of its short lifetime. Built by Sir George Morton, it was improved and repaired in 1729 by the father of Edmund Morton-Pleydell. The house, 'a large handsome pile of a building, surrounded with groves and avenues of trees, pleasant gardens, pieces of water, and every thing that could contribute to elegance and convenience' [Hutchins], was taken down in 1802 when the family moved to Whatcombe. The area of the village where the house stood is called Churcheston. All that remains are two forlorn pillars (the former gateway, whose escutcheoned capitals were removed to the entrance at Whatcombe), and the 80-foot obelisk on the hill lying to the south, now completely hidden by woodland.

A number of names on 'Portland Isle' are of interest, since some appear for the first time on a county map. Kings Key and New Pier appear first on Robert Rowe's map in the previous chapter, but New Key is a new addition and Langley and Belch mention the Old Castle (i.e. Rufus Castle, sited near old St. Andrew's Church), the only time that I have seen this on a map apart from on a 1710 engraving of the Isle of Portland in Hutchins' *History of Dorset*.

The atlas was re-issued in 1820 by Joseph Phelps. He corrected the imprint to read 'Printed and Published by J. Phelps' and amended the dates to read 1820. The atlas was not re-issued after this date and possibly because the editions were not large the maps are quite scarce. The series marks a printing watershed because it was one of the last to carry decorative features done in copper-plate engraving, most subsequent printing plates being engraved on steel or lithographed.

POST OFFICE CIRCULATION MAP, 1823

Maps and postal history are closely interwoven, because roads, once they were shown on maps from the early 1700s, were a useful guide to distance and location, not only for travellers but also for the mail coaches. Originally the post was the exclusive preserve of the government-run Royal Mail, although a blind eye was turned on post-boys carrying private letters to augment their low pay. The first publicly available post was probably on the West Road to Plymouth, introduced by Samuel Jude, in about 1626. This was in competition with the postmasters' monopoly of the hire of horses and carriage of private letters, on which they relied for a reasonable income.

A key figure in the next chapter of the development of the public post was Thomas Hutchins, postmaster at Crewkerne, a stage on the West Road. With Jude in competition and postmasters specifically excluded from making special journeys with private letters, in 1629 Hutchins approached the Privy Council, offering an income to replace the considerable drain on the royal purse. He received permission to undertake the 'speedy dispatch of all private letters weekly from London to Plymouth and from Plymouth to London, and the delivery of letters upon the road, and 20 miles out of the road if need shall require.'

Thus was laid the foundation of the public post, plying its way back and forth along the West Road through North Dorset. Indeed, a number of postmasters on the West Road ran a private foot post from outlying towns to link with the London post. Between 1635 and 1660 five more post roads from London were established (to Dover, Norwich, Edinburgh, Bristol and Dublin). In 1680 the London Local Post, otherwise known as the London Penny Post, was founded by London merchant William Dockwra, who saw opportunity in the fact that no post was provided within cities – one could send a letter by post to Edinburgh, but not inside London. The Penny Post (i.e. a standard penny rate for sending a letter within a ten mile radius of the Cornhill in the city) had a huge impact on postal development thereafter, with provincial Penny Posts being set up in several cities across the country.

The 1801 Postage Act in the reign of George III increased all postage rates, but included the most important 'fifth clause',

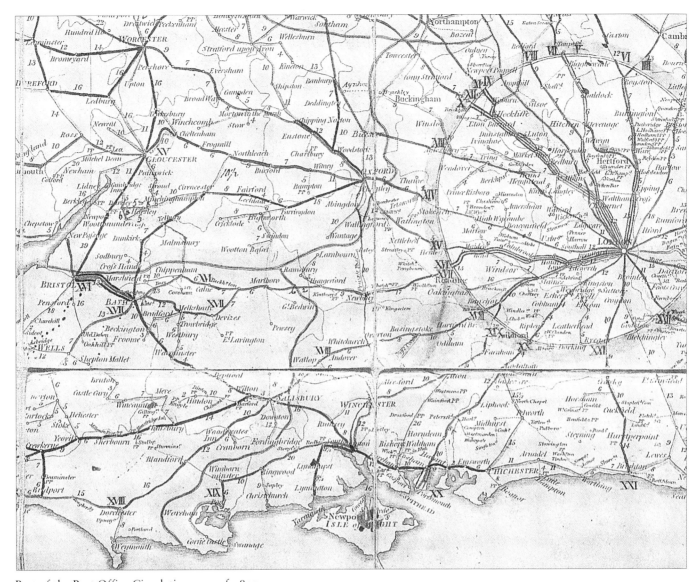

Part of the Post Office Circulation map of 1823.

which allowed the Postmaster-General 'to collect or deliver, to places that are not post towns, letters at such charges as are agreed with the inhabitants.' Thus the private arrangement run by the postmasters on the West Road became official, foreshadowing the establishment of a countrywide postal service. For example, the Shaftesbury to Hindon service opened in 1805, a penny either way, and that between Blandford and Sturminster Newton began in 1807, also at a penny a letter.

Complications arose over 'open boxes' (slits in the walls of receiving houses, through which people could slip outward mail into a locked box, the cost being paid by the recipient). It was the widespread acceptance of the postage stamp that caused open boxes to be used increasingly for prepaid post, until eventually they were made compulsory, resulting in the now familiar red pillar-box. The oldest still in use in Great Britain is at Barnes Cross in Holwell, near Sherborne, which bears Queen

A swan supports both Dorset and Somerset in this French map of 1823.

Victoria's cipher and was manufactured in the 1850s.

The *Post Office Circulation Map of England and Wales*, measuring 560 mm x 620 mm, published in 1823, is a fascinating insight into early nineteenth century postal routes. The Penny Post was a local rate within a defined area such as Metropolitan London. Outside that area a scale of charges applied, based on distance. The map tells us that in 1823, the basic rate for a single letter not exceeding 15 miles was 4d, with a sliding scale of charges for greater distances.

The Roman numerals denote the twenty-three mail coach roads from London, radiating out in an anti-clockwise direction from no. I (Essex Road to Yarmouth) to no. XXIII (Kent Road to Dover). The mail coach roads to Dorset were no. XVIII (to Plymouth via Blandford, Dorchester and Exeter) and no. XIX (to Poole via Winchester, Ringwood and Wimborne).

The West Road through Shaftesbury and Sherborne is marked as a 'cross road' mail coach route. All the local Penny Post services were by foot messenger or on horseback. In Dorset there were four 'daily horse posts' – Woodyates Inn to Cranborne; Shaftesbury to Gillingham; Dorchester to Weymouth; and Poole to Swanage. There was also one 'horse post not daily' from Blandford to Wimborne Minster. Foot messenger deliveries were made in Stalbridge, Henstridge Ash and Milborne Port on the West Road, and in Sturminster Newton, Upwey, Beaminster and Lyme Regis on mail coach road no. XVIII.

ARISTIDE MICHEL PERROT, 1823

This extraordinarily decorative map (see opposite page) is a charming combination of cartography and art. Measuring only 110 mm x 80 mm, it nonetheless provides a surprising amount of accurate detail. The engraving on copper plate, by Madame Migneret, is exceptionally fine.

The maps were originally published by Aristide Michel Perrot in 1823 in a six-volume French work, though a further issue in the same year and a subsequent one in 1835 are without dates. The work is entitled *L'Angleterre ou Description Historique et Topographique du Royaume de la Grand-Bretagne*. The author was Georges Bernard Deeping and the geographical research was done by Perrot himself.

The maps have original hand-colouring and, apart from the playing cards maps mentioned elsewhere, are probably amongst the most unusual miniature county maps ever published. They are sometimes known as the 'gravestone series', because of the uncanny resemblance some of them bear to a headstone.

Fortunately, the map of Dorset does not fall into this category, although the names Somerset and Dorset do appear to be carved on a monumental block of Purbeck marble below the map. A beady-eyed swan with strangely unwebbed feet sits atop a roll-up chart, which is suspended on a cord from its beak. The chart shows the whole of Somerset and Dorset as well as parts of Devon and Wiltshire (the latter abbreviated to 'Wilt' by removing the 'shire' as for the other counties). Glamorgan appears on the north side of the 'Canal de Bristol', and to the south the sea is named 'Baie Exeter'.

The rural nature of Somerset and Dorset is emphasised by the cider jug, the barley for brewing, the fish, the game and the Poole Bay oysters adorning the foreground. Maps from this series are very rare, which, combined with their strongly aesthetic quality, makes them a highly desirable addition to a collection.

CHRISTOPHER AND JOHN GREENWOOD
1825-26, 1829

Famous for their series of large-scale maps printed between 1819 and 1834, the Greenwood brothers were surveyors and publishers who undertook surveys of most of the counties of England and Wales. Amongst these was a cumbersome, canvas-mounted, folding map of Dorset, measuring 1550 mm x 1140 mm and produced 'from an Actual Survey Made in the Years 1825 & 1826 By C and J Greenwood, Most Respectfully Dedicated to the Nobility, Clergy, & Gentry of the County.' It was engraved on 48 panels on a scale of one inch to the mile and was published in 1826 with original hand colouring by Greenwood Pringle and Co. in London, setting new standards for large-scale surveys. The only other large-scale map of the county ever published was Isaac Taylor's survey of 1765 (see page 52).

Although railways are mentioned in the key to the symbols, this map pre-dates the era of public railways and the only

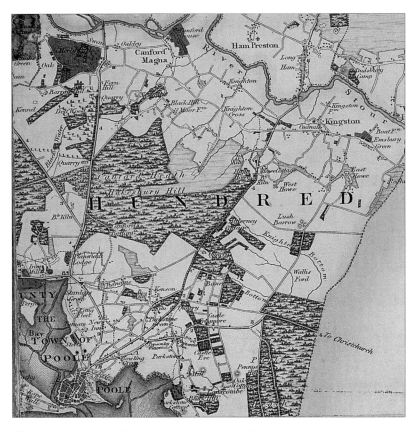

The Poole section of the Greenwoods' large scale map.

reference to a railway is on the Isle of Purbeck, marked 'Iron Railway', as on the 1811 Ordnance Survey map. This was built for the thriving clay trade, serving the half dozen clay pits nearby and transporting the raw product to Middlebere Quay for shipment. Clay from Purbeck is still Poole's main export.

The detail selected for illustration (one panel, measuring 260 mm x 150 mm) shows part of Poole Harbour and the Borough of Poole. The absence of any distinction between the sea and Hampshire means that, at first glance, the blank part on the right looks like the sea. At this scale, individual streets can be made out, and it is interesting to compare it with the 1774 town plan from 55 years earlier (see page 65).

Canford Heath takes up a considerable amount of the space in the centre, and at the top the River Stour flows past Canford House (now Canford School). Poole Heath is to be seen in the lower right-hand corner. Of particular interest is the number of

kilns and quarries, where clay for bricks and stone for building were an important local commodity, from which sprang the Borough's architectural splendour. Among the industries associated with the port were shipbuilding and the manufacture of sails, nets, salt and ropes, though Bridport continued to be the main producer of nets.

In the extreme left-hand corner at Hamworthy is a 'Rope Walk', one of three on the outskirts of the town, producing cordage for local shipping as well as fulfilling government contracts. Marine cable used to be made by men who would walk backwards from a fixed point, twisting the hemp as they went from a bag of loose fibres tied around their waists, until they reached a T-shaped mark indicating the desired length. At the other end operators (often the men's wives) would turn the handle of a mechanism which twisted the fibres together. The process was a repetitive, cumulative one, starting with the fibres twisted clockwise (or Z-laid) which became yarn (experienced operators could make 300 metres in 12 minutes); the yarn was then twisted anti-clockwise (or S-laid) into twine; the twine was Z-laid into line; the line S-laid into rope; and the rope Z-laid into cable. This process ensured that the end product did not have a tendency to coil up of its own accord, very important for all users, especially on board ship. Rope (or Spinning) Walks are also to be found in Bridport and other places around the coast.

The Greenwoods' maps were masterpieces of surveying and their accuracy is remarkable, considering the speed at which they were completed. Technically speaking, their maps exceeded the already high standards of the previous century, although they omitted the decoration and ornate title-pieces that are associated with large-scale maps of that earlier period.

Another series of maps, not large-scale, but based on the same 1825-6 survey, was produced by the Greenwood brothers between 1829 and 1832 in an *Atlas of the Counties of England* (in four parts). The Dorset example, dated 1829, is a very handsome map, measuring 695 mm x 580 mm, reduced to about a quarter of the size of the large-scale map. It is described in the stylishly written title cartouche as 'corrected to the present period' and the claim seems to be justified. The roads are completely up-to-date and several of the major roads outside the county are shown, such as the entire West Road from Salisbury

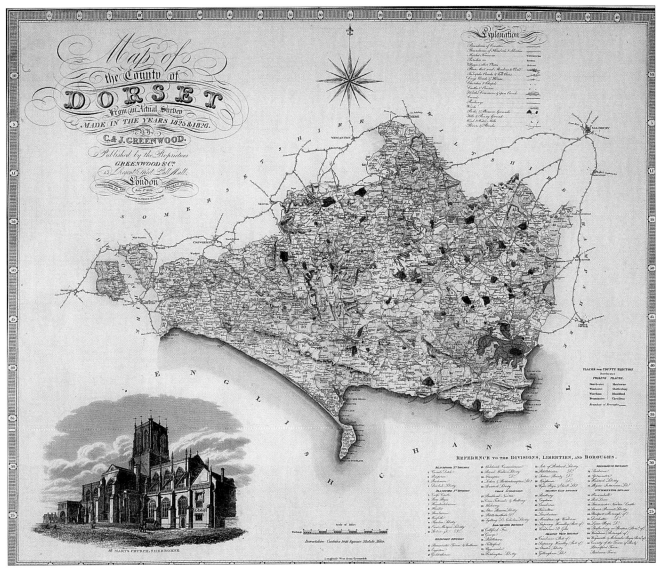

C. & J. Greenwood, 1829.

to Honiton, including distances between towns. On the right-hand side of the map, Salisbury to Christchurch via Downton, Fordingbridge and Ringwood is also shown. There are over forty 'Parks & Pleasure Grounds' (country seats), each highlighted in dark green. In the lower left-hand corner there is a finely engraved view of 'St. Mary's Church, Sherborne' (Sherborne Abbey). The engraver was H. Frost, of 37, Goswell Road, London (near the Barbican).

This is an important map, based on an accurate survey and exceptionally well engraved. Because it is large, the average collector tends to avoid it, but there are examples to be found around the county in public buildings (there is one in the Dorset Rural Music School in Blandford) and in many of the larger country houses. The maps in the series were published coloured, although a second impression of the whole atlas appeared in 1834, with uncoloured maps.

JAMES PIGOT, 1829

The business of James Pigot and Co. flourished during the first half of the nineteenth century, working from premises in London and Manchester. His most famous work is his *British Atlas*, the first steel-engraved atlas ever produced, which he published in 1829. The forty-one maps were engraved to a superlatively high standard, each incorporating a view of a relevant sight or building, in Dorset's case that of 'Sherborne Church', or Sherborne Abbey. The same maps were issued from about 1826 in his *London and Home Counties Directories*.

The Dorset example measures 348 mm x 222 mm and is densely packed with information. Some new properties have appeared since Langley and Belch's map a decade earlier, many built by the new rural ruling class, whose fortunes had been made out of trade and industry. We now see Lewston House, near Sherborne; Motcomb House (called Palmers Place on the Greenwoods' large-scale map) and Pensbury House, near Shaftesbury; Ranston and Stepleton House, near Iwerne Courtney; Langton House, Down House and Turnworth House, near Blandford Forum; Whatcomb House, near Milton Abbas; Gaunts House, High Hall and Uddens House, near Wimborne;

James Pigot, 1829. From his *British Atlas*, the first steel-engraved atlas ever produced.

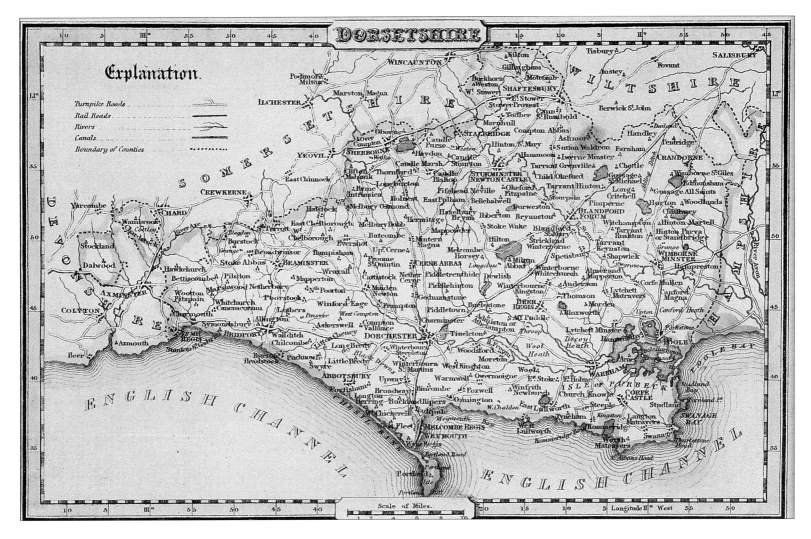

James Pigot's map of Dorset in the *Pocket Topography and Gazetteer of England*, 1838. Note the listing of 'Rail Roads' under 'Explanation'. The only one shown is the 3½ mile horse-drawn railway built to carry ball clay from Norden to Middlebeere Quay on the west side of Poole Harbour: it begins near the 'e' of Church Knowle and looks deceptively like a river.

Henbury House, near Corfe Mullen; Bloxworth House; Wool Park, near Morden; Rempston House, near Corfe; Dewlish House, near Milborne St. Andrew (marked Milbourne Churchstone & St. Andrew); Forston House, near Charminster; and Chalmington House, near Cattistock. Milton Park is shown as having a Deer Park. Eastbury Park has reappeared, whereas Chettle House is not marked.

The current turnpike roads are all marked and the three mail coach roads through Dorset are given due recognition – the West Road from London to Exeter via Shaftesbury and Sherborne; the Great Western Turnpike from Salisbury to Axminster via Blandford, Dorchester and Bridport; and the Ringwood to Poole mail road via Wimborne. The engraving is of a high standard and (with a magnifying glass) it is easy to pick out the detailed markings of the names of villages, rivers, farms, downs, heaths, woodland and country seats. The railway to Middlebeere Quay is referred to as a 'Rail Road'. For the first time on a small-scale county map Badbury Rings hillfort is not only named, but designated by three broken concentric rings. A new symbol in the key or 'Explanation' is a triangle denoting 'Polling Places'.

In many of his ventures, Pigot joined forces with the printer, Isaac Slater, whose name is first mentioned as the printer of the 1844 edition of the *British Atlas*. Pigot died in 1843 and Slater took over Pigot's business in 1846, publishing a final edition of the *British Atlas* in 1857, calling it *The New British Atlas*. Pigot and Slater also co-operated in the *Pocket Topography and Gazetteer of England*, published in parts from 1838, and completed and published as two volumes in 1841, with a second edition in 1842. Further issues of the *Pocket Topography* were made until at least 1857. The firm continued to issue directories after Slater's death, until it was taken over by *Kelly's Directories* in 1892.

The forty maps in the *Pocket Topography and Gazetteer* are smaller and somewhat less decorative than those in the *British Atlas*, but as the title suggests, they are of a handy size (164 mm x 103 mm). They are also easily available and inexpensive. The Dorset example illustrated, dating from 1839, has a simple yellow wash around the county border, including the coastline. The Channel has a broad blue wash, and the Hampshire border is coloured with a thin blue line. The overall effect is neat and concise.

When space is at a premium, it is interesting to see what is included and what is left out. A seemingly random selection of the chief country seats appears, highlighted in green: Sherborne Park, Eastbury Park, St. Giles House, Moore Critchell House, Horton Park, Uddens House, Turnworth House, Milton Park, Bloxworth House, Dewlish House, Kingston House, Lulworth Castle and Encombe House. The engraver overlooked the shading for Stalbridge Park and so the colourist has missed it too.

The rail road to Middlebeere Quay is difficult to identify, since it is almost indistinguishable from a river. The roads are simply designated 'Turnpike Roads'. Both of Pigot's maps have 'Canals' in the Explanation, although none were ever built in Dorset. Many villages have been omitted, including, for example, Milborne St. Andrew. It is interesting to note that Pigot reverts to the original name Sturminster Newton Castle, as used by Christopher Saxton and other early map-makers.

TITHE MAPS, 1838, 1847

Another reason for mapping was to illustrate the 'Tithe Apportionment'. This payment to the Church by the lay population of one-tenth of all produce (whether crops, animal or industrial goods) had been an established practice for about a thousand years. However, by the 1830s about a quarter of all tithes passed into laymen's hands, and tithes were seen as an increasingly irrelevant charge on village communities. The 1836 Tithe Commutation Act sought to abolish tithes altogether by commuting them into rent charges. The task of calculating the rent fell to the Tithe Commissioners, whilst responsibility for the survey was entrusted to Lieutenant Robert K. Dawson, R.E., whose initial insistence on 'first-class' maps (detailed and accurate enough to serve as legal evidence of boundaries and areas) quickly fell by the wayside when it was realised that many parishes would be unable to afford the cost of a 'first-class' survey (9d an acre), settling instead for 'second-class' maps.

Amongst the first tithe maps to be presented to the Commissioners was a Survey of the United Parishes of Evershot and Frome Saint Quintin made by John Martin in 1838. He produced a 'map or plan' of each of the two parishes, 'adopted agreeably to the provisions of the Act', plus an 'award' headed 'Apportionment of the Rent-Charge in lieu of Tithes.' The one of Evershot, the larger of the two, measures 675 mm x 1100 mm, but both are neatly drawn, with houses colour-washed in red on the Frome St. Quintin map and in indigo on the map of Evershot. The scale is 6 chains (approx. 120 metres) to the inch.

Apart from some general remarks, the 34 sheets of the award contain detailed descriptions of the properties, their acreage and state of cultivation, the names of their owners and occupiers, and the amount of rent that was to be charged. A large proportion of the land was owned by the Earl of Ilchester, whilst much of the balance belonged to Sir William Oglander, whose principal estates were on the Isle of Wight. A few of the properties are described as 'Tithe Free' and one as 'Prescriptive Payment'.

Two relatives of Benjamin Jesty, the pioneer of smallpox vaccine who lived in Worth Matravers, are listed as occupiers: Thomas Jesty has lifehold tenancy of Roads Meadow and Stall

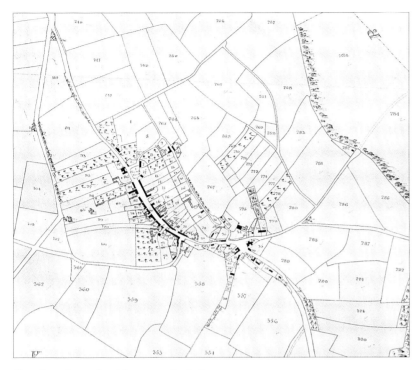

Evershot, from the tithe map of 1838.

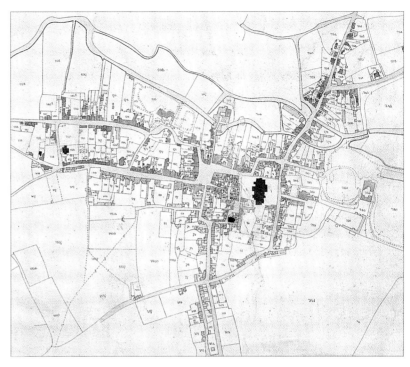

Wimborne Minster, from the tithe map of 1847.

Close, Roads Nine Acres, Roads Six Acres and Roads Four Acres; Anne Jesty, on the other hand, lives in a House with Stable, Garden and Plantation (described as 'Coppice'); that she might have supplied materials to a basket or hurdle-maker is confirmed by her other tenancies, two plots named Yarn Barton and Willow Bed (each with 'Willows' written alongside). John Martin (the surveyor?) occupies a house (no. 16 on the plan). Intriguingly Evershot produced a whole dynasty of surveyors: William Jennings (Senior and Junior), Samuel Donne (see page 57), and John and Edward Martin.

The Commissioners of the Maiden Newton Turnpike owned a house and gardens for the gatekeeper. The Overseers of the Parish provided two houses and gardens for paupers, plus an allotment for fuel. The Waywardens of the Parish had three gravel allotments classified as pasture, but in practice used under Statute Labour as a source of materials for the repair of roads. The Revd. Henry Hoskins was responsible for the Churchyard and some Glebe Land. The award and two maps are stamped with the Commissioners' seal of approval, dated 9/10 Nov. 1840.

A later tithe survey of the Parish of Wimborne Minster is of interest, because it is one of the largest Dorset maps in existence. Measuring 2610 mm x 1690 mm (the size of a large living-room rug), it is housed in the Dorset County Record Office. On a scale of 6 chains to the inch, it was surveyed by J. Poole of Sherborne and bears the official seal of the Tithe Commission (dated July 9 1847) accompanied by the words: 'We the undersigned Tithe Commissioners for England and Wales do hereby certify this to be the map or plan referred to in the Apportionment of the Rent Charge in lieu of tithes in the Parish of Wimborne Minster in the County of Dorset.'

An inset plan (575 mm x 465 mm) of the town of Wimborne Minster takes up part of the survey, providing a clear picture of the layout of the town at that date. The Churches and their properties are prominent on the plan: Plot No. 1 is Wimborne Minster (described in the award as simply 'Church and Yard'); Plot No. 17 belongs to the 'Trustees of the Wesleyan Chapel (Ebenezar Chapel)'; Plot No. 139 to the 'Trustees of the Independent Chapel & Garden'; and Plot No. 134 (Cottages and

Garden) belonging also to the latter trustees. The open circular space to the right of the Minster is Plot No. 280, 'Deans Court, offices, yard, gardens and pleasure grounds', occupied at that time by the Reverend Sir James Hanham.

As with estate and enclosure maps and their awards, the whole map with its numbered plots must be read in conjunction with the accompanying Tithe Apportionment books, which (like the Evershot award sheets) are full of the names of the local landowners. The Apportionment books can present a daunting prospect to would-be researchers, because they are in groups of land and property holdings, not in numerical order. However, in this case, the Record Office has made a transcript which is in numerical order, making the identification of the numbered plots on the map a relatively easy task. Chief amongst the landowners, unsurprisingly, was George Bankes Esq. of Kingston Hall (Kingston Lacy). Unexpectedly, another substantial landowner in the parish of Wimborne Minster was Sherborne School.

Tithe maps are an important part of rural history because they contain examples of every type of land holding, from scattered plots in the remaining open fields to the great estates of the landed proprietors. Prior to Tithe Commutation, many owners accepted (as in the Walditch Inclosure Commissioners Award, see page 73) a once-for-all allotment of land in lieu of receipt of tithes. Some remarkable bargains were obtained, since there was no question of receiving allotments of as little as one-tenth of the titheable land. Towards the end of the eighteenth century and at the beginning of the nineteenth, one-fifth of the arable land and one-ninth of the pasture were normally ceded to the new owners in such cases.

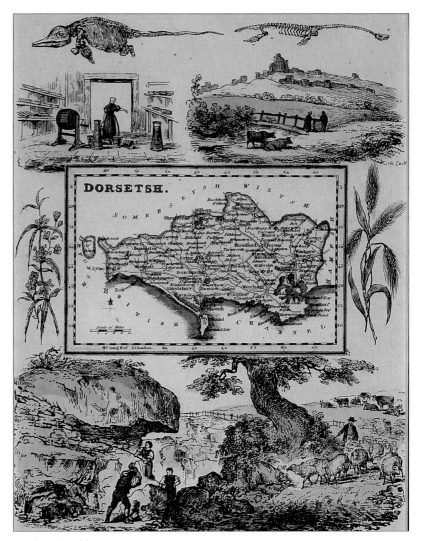

Reuben Ramble, 1845.

REUBEN RAMBLE, 1845

Reuben Ramble published his charming school atlas *Travels through the Counties of England* in 1845. It was the only printing and, not surprisingly, copies of the maps are rare. There were forty lithographed maps in all, which had first appeared thirty-five years earlier in Miller's *New Miniature Atlas*. Each county is surrounded by views associated with its way of life. They take up more space than the map itself, which measures 105 mm x 70 mm.

According to Ramble, Dorset is famous for fossils, farming and stone quarrying. In the top left hand corner, a milkmaid carries a pail out of a cheese-making room. At the top right, there is a peaceful rural scene with Corfe Castle in the background. Below, a shepherd drives his flock towards some men cleaving stone in a quarry. The herd of cows brings to mind the dairy farms of the Blackmore Vale. Either side of the map are two of the arable products of Dorset: to the left, flax for the manufacture of linen, and to the right, barley for foodstuffs and brewing.

The contemporary colourist of this particular example has given the quarrymen smart blue waistcoats, but was evidently no botanist, painting the flowers of the flax with an insipid pink wash, instead of the brilliant blue they deserve. At the top, there are drawings of an ichthyosaur and a plesiosaur, a tribute to Mary Anning's first discovery and identification of these remarkable fossils, found by her in the lias at Lyme Regis in 1811.

SAMUEL LEWIS AND
JOHN AND CHARLES WALKER, 1845

Samuel Lewis was a draughtsman, cartographer and publisher, who traded under the name of S. Lewis & Co. He is best known for his series of topographical dictionaries of England, Wales, Scotland and Ireland, all of which had maps specially produced to accompany the relevant volumes. The first of the dictionaries was published in four volumes in 1831, entitled the *Topographical Dictionary of England*, containing forty-three maps, including one of England and Wales, as well as a plan of London. The maps are all drawn by R. Creighton. Some are engraved by T. Starling, but most, as in the case of the Dorset map, by the brothers John and Charles Walker, who were publishers as well as prolific engravers.

The Dorset example, measuring 230 mm x 170 mm, is from a later edition in 1845 and is an accurate and finely engraved map. All the latest roads are included, delineated with a firm line when enclosed with hedges or fences, and a dotted line when open over heaths or commons. The many churches are marked with a cross.

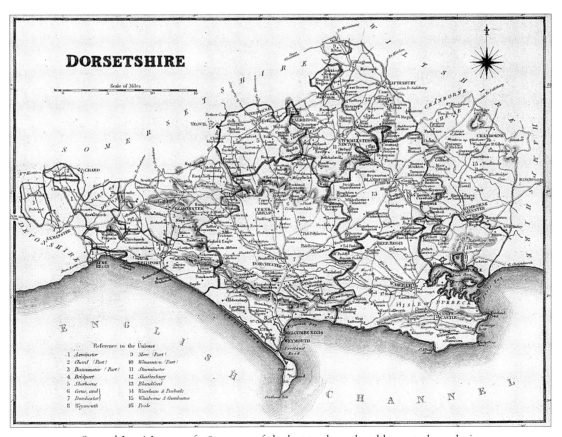

Samuel Lewis's map of 1845, one of the last to show the old county boundaries.

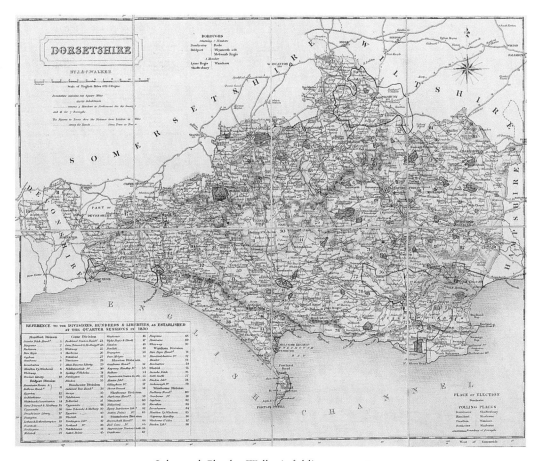

John and Charles Walker's folding map, 1841.

The map abandons the depiction of country seats, and breaks new ground by showing the Unions, which were a consequence of the Poor Law Amendment Act of 1834. The Act abolished the old system of Poor Relief managed by Parish Overseers (which had begun in the reign of Queen Elizabeth I) and Poor Law Commissioners were appointed to introduce a new system of Poor Law Unions (aggregations of two or more parishes) run by Boards of Guardians.

The Guardians, elected by local landowners and rate-payers, took over the responsibility for poor relief. They built new workhouses, with a strict regime for the inmates. Not intended to be attractive, the workhouses were harsh places, more like penitentiaries than sanctuaries. The genuinely needy were forced to enter an environment designed to repel malingerers, who, it was hoped, would find gainful employment.

This decade of crucial political reform also saw the passing of the Great Reform Act of 1832, which decreed a substantial redistribution of political seats, and reduced Dorset's number of M.P.s to fourteen from twenty. This was still more than twice the appropriate allocation based on population, an imbalance which was finally removed when the number was reduced to four, one for each division. Only in 1948 did Poole again become a parliamentary borough, regaining two seats because of its greatly increased population.

Lewis' 1845 map was one of the last to show the old county boundaries, a feature of many of the maps in this book. In 1844, the boundaries were redrawn, clearing up some of the long-standing anomalies. Stockland and Dalwood in the far west were officially declared part of Devon, while the parish of Thorncombe was transferred to Dorset. Holwell parish, the outlying part of Somerset first mentioned in the chapter on Saxton, was declared to be part of Dorset. A further tidying up of boundaries occurred in 1896, when the parishes of Trent, Poyntington, Sandford Orcas, Goathill and Seaborough were transferred from Somerset to Dorset. Chardstock and Hawkchurch passed to Devon, and Wambrook passed to Somerset.

The Topographical Dictionary went into many editions, with the imprint 'Drawn and Engraved for Lewis' Topographical Dictionary' appearing on every map. The second edition was published in 1833, and there were further editions published in 1835, 1840, 1842, 1845, with a final edition in 1849.

The other example of John and Charles Walker's work, published in 1841, breaks new ground as a genuinely pocket-sized folding map, unlike the Ordnance Survey folding maps, which were more suited to the large pockets of a military greatcoat. The map itself measures 398 mm x 322 mm and packs a huge amount of information into a very small space. Folded, the paper-on-linen map measures a mere 104 mm x 173 mm. All the main roads of the day are shown, including, at last, the continuation of the road (from Horton) crossing the Harnham, Blandford and Dorchester Turnpike to Shaftesbury. Distances from London are shown in miles, and large numbers of minor roads are also shown.

There is a profusion of country seats, with some being marked for the first time on a map of this size, for example, Parnham House, near Beaminster, and others making their first appearance on a map of any kind, for example, Dean's Leaze, near Witchampton and Hethfelton, near East Stoke. On the death of the last occupant of Dean's Leaze (Major-General Sir George Bingham), the mansion was bought and pulled down by Humphrey Sturt, owner of Crichel, and the stables converted into a farm house. Hethfelton, referred to as Heffleton in Hutchins' *History of Dorset*, was built by Dr. Andrew Bain, 'who greatly beautified and improved the estate by plantations and ornamental grounds. The former were so extensive that he was presented in 1808 with a gold medal by the Society of Planting, as an honorary testimonial.'

Some general information is given in the key, namely, that Dorsetshire contains 1211 Square Miles, has 159,252 Inhabitants, returns 3 Members to Parliament for the County and 11 for 7 Boroughs.

THOMAS MOULE, 1850

Thomas Moule was an accomplished, London-based authority on heraldry and antiquities, as well as being a map-seller and publisher. Late in the reign of William IV he prepared a highly decorative set of maps of the English counties, published in 1837 by George Virtue, containing fifty-eight city plans and county maps. The two-volume atlas was called *The English Counties Delineated*, and its maps have long had an enduring appeal, because of the elaborate decorations. Each map had a set of armorials and charming vignette views, as well as symbolic figures, ornate stone tracery or foliate embellishment.

There was another edition of *The English Counties Delineated* in 1837, and a third edition came out in 1838. The identical maps appeared, but without Moule's imprint, in a long-running publication, *Barclay's Dictionary*. This work was named after the Rev. James Barclay, who used Moule's maps in his work, which was first published without maps in 1840, and then ran into many editions, with maps, until the last one in 1852. This made the maps available to a far greater readership than an atlas is normally exposed to, and their popularity remains undiminished.

This example from *Barclay's Dictionary* of around 1850, measuring 260 mm x 200 mm, is less decorated than some. Nonetheless it has all the hallmarks of Moule – fine engraving, several armorials and a vignette view. In this case the scene is a drawing by George Shepherd, originally engraved by W. Woolnorth and reproduced from *The Beauties of England and Wales*, which was published in 1804. It depicts the Shaftesbury ridge, with St James' and Holy Trinity churches silhouetted on the skyline, and there is a fisherman in the foreground. The coats-of-arms are of the Digby family, and of the town and borough of Dorchester. The seals are of the Abbey of Abbotsbury, and St Edward's Abbey, Shaftesbury.

Thomas Moule, 1850.

As railways were built, they were added to the maps and help to date them. Dorset's public railways date from 1845, when Acts were passed permitting two of the county's four main lines. In this case a line comes in from Southampton via Wareham to Dorchester, built by the Southampton and Dorchester Railway Company, opened in 1847. Branching off to the south, you can see the proposed link to Weymouth, planned by the Bristol and Exeter Company.

The Twentieth Century

County maps continued into the twentieth century, but went into a decline for a number of reasons. The huge network of railways and the advent of the motor car meant that people began to travel further afield and no longer regarded the county as the boundary of their existence. Increasing leisure time and affluence allowed greater movement of population than ever before. British and European road atlases and route planners provided by motoring organisations, or nowadays available on the Internet, have deprived the county map of one of its chief functions.

At the beginning of the nineteenth century travel was still the preserve of the well-to-do, but by the mid-1800s, the walking map was popular in Victorian England. The advent of the railway had opened up the countryside to ordinary people, who found that they could travel relatively cheaply to hitherto distant parts of the country for walking trips. As a healthy hobby, walking soon became a fad and the early 'Railway Traveller' and 'Walker' maps were produced to cater for the new activity. Books of walks with their own maps have become increasingly popular. One of the most recent of these is the Jarrold Publishing Pathfinder Guide *Dorset Walks*, using Ordnance Survey maps on a scale of 1:25,000 and produced in the 1990s. It has gone into several reprints and is one of the clearest and most comprehensive guides available.

With the invention of the mass-produced bicycle, the walking map evolved into the cycling map. Most were taken from resurrected Ordnance Survey plates and were intended to be functional rather than decorative, but the covers were often a cheerful contrast to the contents. *Bacon's Dorset County Map and Guide for Tourists and Cyclists*, a folding map published in

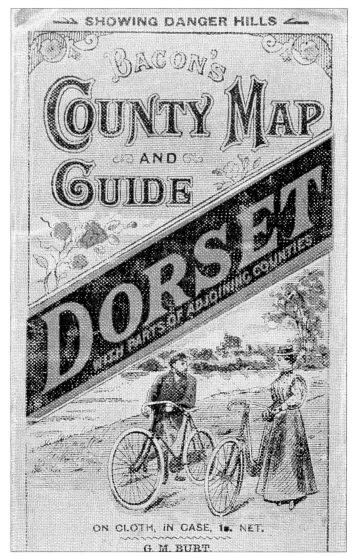

The cover of an early map aimed at cyclists, published in 1904.

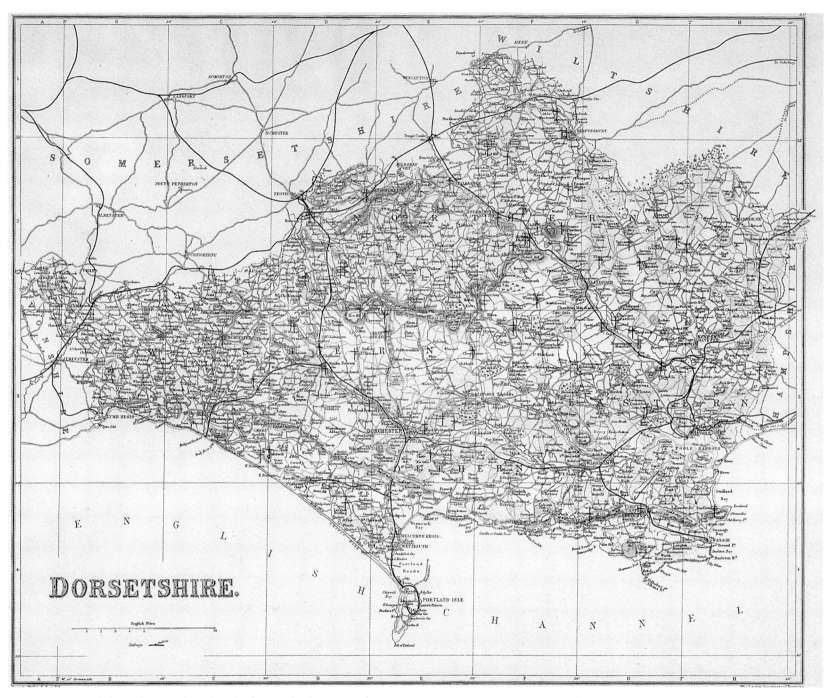

In 1920 George Philip and Son Ltd produced a fine single sheet map of Dorset, measuring 415 mm x 335 mm, showing its entire railway network. By this time, there were branch lines to such outlying places as Lyme Regis, Abbotsbury, Verwood and Easton on the Isle of Portland. Dorset's railway network was then at its peak; 170 miles of track were served by 67 stations and halts.

The Chideock Parish Map, painted by Gillian Moores in 1990 (see page 98).

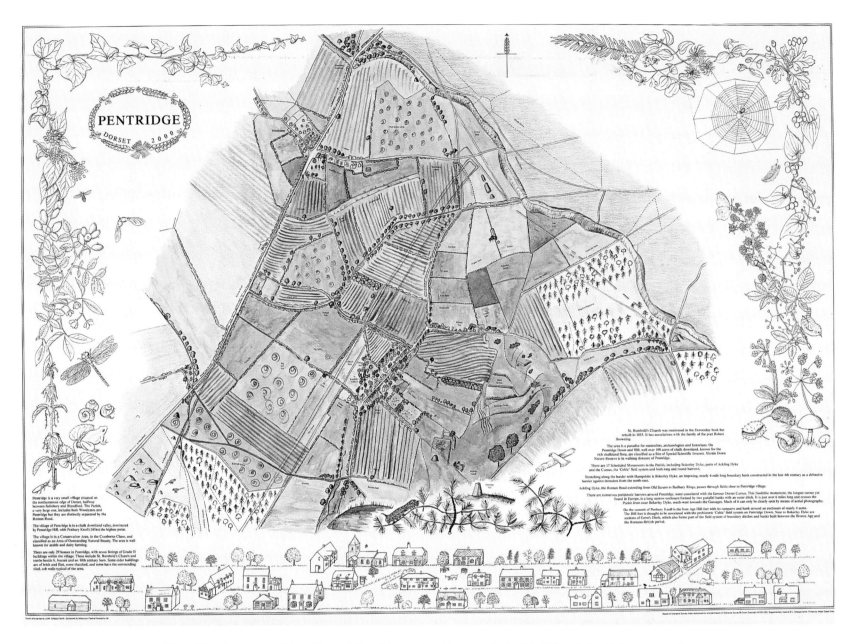

The millennium map of the village of Pentridge, painted in 2000 by Judith Gillespie-Smith (see page 98).

1904, depicts on the cover a couple dressed in Edwardian cycling garb ready for an invigorating ride through their picturesque county, in complete confidence of not losing their way (or indeed their balance, since 'Danger Hills' are identified with a single feather pointing down hills that had to be ridden with caution and double feathers for those that were dangerous). *Bacon's Cycling Map* was first published around 1883 and went into many editions over the next few decades.

Probably the most famous map of the Dorset area, and the most inaccurate, is the map that Thomas Hardy himself created

– Thomas Hardy's Wessex – to accompany the 1912 Wessex Edition of his novels and which is reproduced in subsequent editions. Hardy himself said of *A Laodicean* that 'its sites, mileages, and architectural details can hardly seem satisfactory to the investigating topographist, so appreciable a proportion of these features being but the baseless fabrics of a vision.' The map and the novels can provide a fascinating study for the Hardy enthusiast comparing fictitious names with their real counterparts. For the reader bent on investigating the topography of the novels, there is Hermann Lea's *Thomas Hardy's Wessex*, written with the novelist's help.

An important function of map-making has always been its strategical use in planning national defence. The Ordnance Survey played a key role in this respect, never more so than in the twentieth century. In time of war military intelligence has recognised the value of information about the enemy in map form. In 1944, as the Allies took Belgium from the retreating German Army, it became clear from captured material that from well before the outbreak of the Second World War the German authorities had been busy acquiring British and Irish Ordnance Survey maps for future use in military operations. Sometimes sensitive information can be suppressed on civilian maps, and since the middle of the nineteenth century the War Office has enforced rules about what can be shown.

In the Keep Military Museum in Dorchester there is a large wall-map compiled by the Dorset Constabulary pinpointing all bombs and crashed aircraft which fell in the county during the 1939 – 1945 war. It is a remarkable record; prime targets were airfields (such as Henstridge, Warmwell and Tarrant Rushton), factories (such as Whitehead's Torpedo Works at Ferrybridge and the Royal Naval Cordite Factory at Holton Heath) and installations (such as the Air Ministry's top secret Telecommunications and Research Establishment at Worth Matravers). The latter's importance to the war effort cannot be underestimated. In January 1944 Swanage had more air raid alerts than London, prompting Churchill's order: 'Move before the next full moon!' His word was their command. Very swiftly the TRE installation was moved to Great Malvern and Dorset was spared one of its sensitive wartime targets.

Air raid damage to some of Dorset's key military installations was significantly reduced by one of the country's best-kept secrets. 'Q-sites' were mock installations to draw enemy fire away from the real thing. Craftsmen from Denham Film Studios, sworn to secrecy, were employed to build at Chickerell full-size replicas of the Portland oil tanks. Complete with subdued compound lighting, they fooled the German pilots into bombing the fake tanks. After the first strike, fires of coal, rags, paraffin and diesel oil were set alight by remote control from underground bunkers, so that when the second wave came through, it appeared that the target had been hit, therefore more bombs were dropped on the same site. So successful was this ploy that the oil tanks at Portland (despite German claims to the contrary) remained intact throughout the war.

In 1994 The Wartime Company of Bournemouth produced *Dorset in Wartime*, a map celebrating the fiftieth anniversary of D-Day. Measuring 840 mm x 590 mm, it shows the location of the administrative centres (camps, HQs, SOE, Military Engineering Establishments, Gun Operations Rooms and Hospitals) and the key military installations throughout the county at the time of the Normandy landings.

The map drawers and cabinets of the County Reference Library in Dorchester are well worth a visit. As well as many of the antique maps mentioned in this book, the Library has twentieth century maps covering many areas of interest (for a list of some of the key twentieth century maps in the County Reference Library see *Further Reading*).

The County Reference Library also holds the entire series of Ordnance Survey sheets covering Dorset at a scale of 25 inches to the mile. These were the largest scale maps the Ordnance Survey ever produced, printed and published in 1935, based on the survey for the 1901 Second Edition. There are not far short of a thousand sheets, each the size of a table top. Every detail of the landscape is shown and these became effectively the estate maps of the twentieth century, used by landlords, farmers, councils and surveyors.

Some of the most interesting and decorative maps are those of villages, produced locally by map-makers and artists, sometimes commissioned by parish, or parochial church councils. Many were the result of the 'Parish Maps' projected initiated by Common Ground in the 1980s encouraging villages to identify

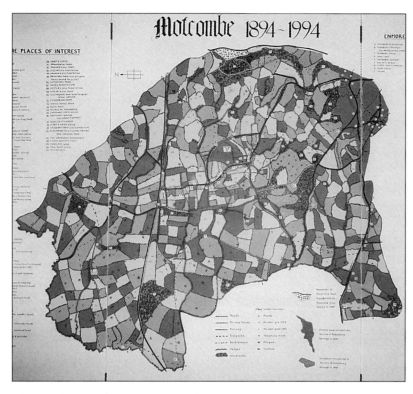

The parish map of Motcombe, which is nearly 8 feet by 6 feet and housed in the Village Hall.

the special character of their own place, and to celebrate and conserve it. They were generally hand-drawn and hand-painted, and were often published in limited editions, such as *The Parish of Lytchett Minster before 1950* by Sylvia May (1986); *The Parish of Uplyme* by Sally Hargreaves, Clare Dell and Christine Cage (1987); and *Church Knowle – The Life of the Parish from earliest times until 1989*, drawn by John Tennent for Church Knowle P. C. C. (1989). Three striking examples of village maps are the parish maps of Chideock in the south-west, Motcombe in north Dorset, and Pentridge in the east.

Painted by Gillian M. Moores in 1990 and measuring 1220 mm x 1220 mm (four feet square), the *Chideock Parish Map* (see page 95) was commissioned by the Chideock Society, formed specifically for this purpose. The project began in 1988 with the posting of a handmade notice asking 'Do you know your place?', and inviting people to come to a village hall meeting, to which

twenty-eight turned up. Known locally as the 'Parish Mappers', they met monthly in each other's homes, organised the photographing of all the streets in the parish and did other topographical research. Two years in the making, the highly decorative map represents the interests and values of the community, not least the desire to preserve Chideock's identity in the face of an influx of tourists and holidaymakers who more than double the population of the coastal village during the summer and autumn. In 1996 the map was one of 28 selected from all over the nation for display, first in the Barbican and subsequently in Bath and Truro.

The Motcombe Parish Map is an exceptional map in the form of a triptych mural measuring 2370 mm x 1800 mm (nearly 8 feet by 6 feet). Designed and drawn in 1994 by members of a Parish Council sub-committee, it celebrates the Council's centenary, and is housed in Motcombe Memorial Hall. The map contains the whole parish and the key shows, amongst other things, field names, places of interest, ponds, watercourses, houses pre-1939 and post-1945, telephone kiosks, mileposts and postboxes.

The final example of the map-maker's art brings us to the Millennium and reminds us that, as for our forbears, our awareness of our place in the world and our desire to record it remain undiminished. Measuring 840 mm x 590 mm and completed in November 2000 by local artist Judith Gillespie-Smith, the map of the village of Pentridge (see page 96) was commissioned by the Village Hall Committee thanks to a Lottery Millennium Festival Award. As a retired entomologist from Reading University, Gillespie-Smith has the eye for detail which has enabled the scheme to have such a successful outcome. Her map is a remarkable result of careful research and painstaking effort, showing land use, wildlife, archaeology, and all the houses in the village. That such a project was undertaken at all is a tribute to the will of many parishioners, who provided photographs, information on field names and completed questionnaires, recording the features which they felt characterised the village. It is a certainty that such projects will continue to be inititiated elsewhere in the country. Therein lies the strength of the cartographic tradition.

Acknowledgements

I am indebted to John Booth, whose book *Looking at Old Maps* has been my chief guide over the years that I have been collecting, and to Yasha Beresiner, whose book *British County Maps* has been an invaluable source of reference. I have also made frequent use of Thomas Chubb's *The Printed Maps in the Atlases of Great Britain and Ireland 1579 – 1870.* These and other sources of reference are listed under Further Reading. Nick Millea of the Bodleian Library and Peter Barber and Geoff Armitage of the British Library have provided me with useful information.

I owe a special debt of thanks to the Reproductions Department of the British Library for kindly granting permission for the reproduction of Henry VIII's *Bird's-Eye View of the Dorset Coast* (Cott. Mss. Augustus 1, i, 31 & 33) and the late sixteenth century map of Portland and Weymouth attributed to Robert Adams (Cott. Mss. Augustus 1, i, 32).

I am extremely grateful to Peter Irvine and David Reeve of the Dorset County Record Office in Dorchester for assisting me in my research, and to the County Archivist, Hugh Jaques, for allowing the inclusion of maps from the Record Office Collection: namely Isaac Taylor's wonderful large-scale map of 1765, the Corscombe Estate Map of 1799, the enclosure map of Walditch of 1810, C & J Greenwood's map of 1825-6, and the Tithe maps of Evershot (1838) and Wimborne Minster (1847),

The National Trust kindly granted permission to reproduce Ralph Treswell's *Survey of the Isle of Purbeck,* 1586, and details from the Kingston Lacy Estate Maps of 1742 and 1773. Nearly all the maps in the book were photographed by Paul Lipscombe and I am grateful to him for the high quality of the transparencies.

Kate Geraghty, the prime mover in the mapping of Chideock, has been immensely helpful, as have a number of Motcombe parishioners. Judith Gillespie-Smith kindly agreed to the reproduction of her millennium map of the village of Pentridge. The environmental arts charity Common Ground has helpfully supplied background information about the 'Parish Maps' project.

I owe many thanks to my wife, Sally, who has patiently typed and proof-read my manuscripts and given me helpful advice, and to my children, Michael and Caroline, who have also read my manuscripts and made many suggestions which I have incorporated into the text. I am particularly grateful to Dr Geoffrey Tapper, Dr David Brewin and his son Mark, who have freely loaned maps and books. Similarly I am grateful to Peter James for loaning reference books, many of which are out of print. Finally, I would like to thank David Burnett for his guidance and encouragement, which led to the unearthing of much of historical interest about Dorset.

Further Reading

Barber, Peter and Board, Christopher, *Tales from the Map Room* (BBC Books), 1993

Baynton-Williams, Roger, *Investing in Maps* (Barrie & Rockliff, The Cresset Press), 1969

Beresiner, Yasha, *British County Maps* (Antique Collectors' Club), 1983

Bettey, J.H., *Dorset* (David & Charles), 1974

Bettey, J.H., *Farming* (The Dovecote Press), 2000

Bond, William H., *Assertor of Liberty, Citizen of the World*, paper on Thomas Hollis by the Professor of Bibliography at Harvard (Librarian of Houghton Library), 1974

Booth, John, *Looking at Old Maps* (Cambridge House Books), 1979

Browne, Robert, Col., *Daily Journal,* unpublished family archive, 1802

Chacksfield, K. Merle, *Smuggling Days* (Dorset Publishing Company) 3rd. edition, 1984

Chubb, Thomas, *The Printed Maps in the Atlases of Great Britain and Ireland 1579-1870* (William Dawson & Sons Ltd.) 3rd. impression, 1977

Conduit, Brian, *Pathfinder Guide Dorset Walks* (Jarrold-OS), 1992, reprinted 1995/6

Cowan, James, *A Mapmaker's Dream* (Sceptre), 1997

Cowie, Leonard W., *Hanoverian England 1714-1837* (G.Bell & Son Ltd.), 1967

Cullingford, Cecil N., *A History of Poole* (Phillimore), 1988

Dorset Wildlife Trust, *The Natural History of Dorset* (The Dovecote Press), 1997

Fägersten, Anton, *The Place Names of Dorset* (EP Publishing Limited), 1978. First published 1933, (Uppsala University, Sweden)

Feltwell, John, *The Naturalist's Garden* (Templar Publishers Ltd), 1987

Forty, George, *Frontline Dorset, A County at War 1939-45* (Dorset Books), 1994

Fowles, John and Draper, Jo, *Thomas Hardy's England* (Jonathan Cape Ltd), 1984

Gambier, Jennifer, *Tithe Free Districts in Dorset at the Time of Tithe Commutation,* Somerset and Dorset Notes and Queries, Vol. XXXII, 1990

Good, Ronald, *The Old Roads of Dorset* (Horace G. Commin Ltd., Bournemouth), 1966, new enlarged edition. First published 1940.

Goss, John, *The Mapmaker's Art, An Illustrated History of Cartography* (Rand McNally), 1993

Hindle, Brian Paul, *Maps for Local History* (Batsford), 1988

Hodgkiss, A.G., *Discovering Antique Maps* (Shire Publications Ltd.), 1977, fourth edition, reprinted 1988

Humphreys, A.L., *Antique Maps and Charts* (Dorset Press, New York, Bracken Books), 1989

Hutchins, John, *The History and Antiquities of the County of Dorset* (Bowyer & Nichols), three editions, 1774, 1796-1815 & 1861-70

Hyland, Paul, *Purbeck, The Ingrained Island* (The Dovecote Press), 1989

Innes, Brenda, *Shaftesbury, An Illustrated History* (The Dovecote Press), 1992

Jessel, Christopher, *The Law of the Manor* (Barry Rose Law Publishers Ltd), 1998

Kentish, Brian, *Large Scale County Maps of England and Wales, 1705-1832*, 1997

Lucking, J.H., *Dorset Railways* (The Dovecote Press), 1982

Moreland, Carl and Bannister, David, *Antique Maps* (Phaidon Press), 1983. 3rd. edition, reprinted 1998

Morris, Stuart, *Portland, An Illustrated History* (The Dovecote Press), 1985

Nissel, Muriel, *People Count, A History of the General Registrar* (Crown Copyright, London, HMSO), 1987. Second impression 1989

O'Donoghue, Yolande, *William Roy, 1726-1790: Pioneer of the Ordnance Survey* (British Museum Publications Ltd), 1977

Osborn, George, *Dorset Curiosities* (The Dovecote Press), 1986

Page, William (ed), *A History of the County of Dorset*, Vol 2 (The University of London Institute of Historical Research), 1975

Pomeroy, Colin, *Military Dorset Today* (published by the author in association with Silver Link Publishing Ltd), 1995

Potter, Jonathan, *Country Life Book of Antique Maps* (Country Life), 1988

Proceedings of the Dorset Natural History and Archaeological Society for 1961, Vol. 83; 1964, Vol. 86; 1973, Vol. 95

Proceedings of the Dorset Natural History and Antiquarian Field Club, Volume VII, 1875

Robbins, Caroline, *Thomas Hollis in His Dorsetshire Retirement* (Harvard Library Bulletin, Volume XXIII), 1975

Royal Commission on Historical Monuments, Crown Copyright, *Historical Monuments of the County of Dorset* (HMSO Press, Edinburgh), 1970

Sellman, R.R., *Illustrations of Dorset History* (Methuen), 1960

Skelton, R.A., *Decorative Printed Maps of the 15th to 18th Centuries* (Spring Books, London, 2nd. Impression), 1966

Smith, David, *Maps and plans for the local historian and collector* (Batsford), 1988

Speed, John, *The Counties of Britain, A Tudor Atlas* (Pavilion Books Limited), 1988

Stenton, Sir Frank, *Anglo-Saxon England, Oxford History of England*, 3rd. ed. (Oxford University Press), 1971

Tattersfield, Nigel, *The Forgotten Trade* (Jonathan Cape), 1991 (Pimlico edition), 1998

Traskey, J.P., *Milton Abbey, A Dorset Monastery in the Middle Ages* (Compton Press), 1978

Tooley, R.V., *Maps and Map-Makers* (Batsford), 7th. edition. 1987

The Victoria History, *A History of Dorset*, volume II, 1908 (reprinted 1975)

Willcocks, R.M., *England's Postal History*, 1975

Woodcock, Thomas and Robinson, John Martin, *The Oxford Guide to Heraldry* (Oxford University Press), 1988

The following list is a selection of some of the twentieth century maps in the County Reference Library, Dorchester.

For the geographer: *Land Utilisation Surveys* (1931-32); *The Dorset Landscape* (1935); *Countryside Commission – Landscape Character* (1970s); *River Systems* (1970); *Solid Geology* (1977); *Wessex Water Authority Hydrogeological Map* (1979); *Sea Bed Geology* (1990).

For the rambler and hiker: *Bournemouth Municipal Borough – Definitive Map of Public Rights of Way* (1972); *Ordnance Survey Rights of Way in Dorset*, scale 1:25,000 (1989).

For the yachtsman: Yachting Charts (some pre-war, some from the 1970s).

For the general historian: *Historical Map of Dorset* by Philip N. Dawes (1949); *Dorset* by Roy Faiers (1967).

For the family historian: *Map of Heraldic and Genealogical Studies* (1964).

For the road historian: *Turnpikes and Tollhouses* by John Bartholomew (1970); *Classified County Roads* (1975 & 1986).

For the literary enthusiast: *Dorset – Who's Afeärd?* by J L Carr (1973).

For the tourist: *Kelly's Map of Dorsetshire*, Kelly's Directories Ltd. (1939); *Panorama Map of Central South Coast*, W. & A. K. Johnston & Bacon Ltd. (1950s); *Dorset: Area of Outstanding Natural Beauty*, as confirmed by the Minister of Housing and Local Government (1957); *Whereabouts of the Various Licensed Premises* compiled by K. C. Jordan (1964); *Where to go in Wessex* by C. Stanton (1973); *Pictorial Map of Pleasure and Leisure in Dorset*, Michael Grant Associates (1980); *County of Dorset* (with a simplified map of Thomas Hardy's Wessex on the reverse), Franchise Publications (1990).

Index

The numbers in **bold type** refer to illustrations.

Broadcloth, 25
Broadmayne, 60
Broadwey, 38
Broadwindsor, 60
Brodrepp, Richard, 66
Brown, Lancelot (Capability), 50
Browne, Colonel Robert, 71
Brownsea ("Bruncksey") Island, 9, 10, 11, 40, 46, 65
Bryanston House, 71, **72**
Bryanston Park, 78
Bryanston Place, 63
Bryanston School, 71
Bulbarrow, 50, **51**, 60
Bullion, 54
Burton Bradstock, 11, 44
Butter-making, 66
Button-making, 25, 27, 44
Button Shop, Old, 44

Cable, 82
Cage, Christine, 98
Calcraft, Colonel Thomas, 65
Cambridge University, 76
Camden, William, **16**, 17, 22, 28, 34, 35
Camden's Britannia, 16, 17, 34; *Epitomised & Completed*, 17
Came House, 63
Canals, 86
Canal de Bristol (Bristol Channel), 80, 81
Canford, 12
Canford Heath, 82
Canford House, 82
Canford School, 82
Canford Magna (Canford Great Park), 11, 28
Canford Parva (Canford Little Park), 11, 28
Cann, 30
Canvas, 44
Carpets, 44
Cary, John, 34, 61, **62**, 63, 64; *Cary's New & Correct English Atlas*, **62**; *Cary's New English Atlas*, 63; *Cary's New Map of England and Wales, with Part of Scotland*, **62**; *Cary's Traveller's Companion*, 61, **62**, 63
Case, Abraham, 25, 44
Case, Peter, 44
Cashmoor, 61, 64, 71
Cashmoor Inn, 63
Castle Hill (Shaftesbury), 30
Castles: Lulworth, 28, 57; Maiden, 71; Portland, 10, 14, 15, 22, 23, 28; Rufus (Portland), 78; Sandsfoot, 9, 10, 14, 15, 22, 23, 58; Studland, 15,

62; Sturminster Newton, 86
Casualties (wartime), 97
Cattistock, 48, 85
Cattle, 48, 57, **73**
Cerne Abbas, 44, 48, 64
Chafin, George, 63
Chain (=22 yards), 68, 73, 87
Chalbury, 44
Chalmington House, 85
Channel, The, 46
Channel, Bristol, 81
Channel, English, 43, 62, 86
Channel, British, 62
Channel Islands, 44
Characters, see Conventional Signs
Charborough, 63, 78
Chardstock, 91
Charity Schools, 48; see also Free Schools
Charles I, 16, 25
Charles II, **32**, 33, 48
Charlton Marshall, 38
Charminster, 85
Charmouth, 11
Chase Law, 40
Cheese-making, 88
Chesil Beach (Chesil Bank), 50, **54**
Chesilton, 15
Chettle, 37, 40, 63, 78, 85
Chickerell, 60, 63, 97
Chideock, **95**, 98
Chorographia Britanniae (Badeslade & Toms), **42**, 42-43
Christchurch, 13, 76, 83
Chubb, Thomas, 8
Church Knowle, 98
Church Lane (Bridport), 66
Churcheston (Milborne St.Andrew), 78, 85
Churchhope (Portland), 15
Churchill, John, 34
Churchill, Sir Winston, 97
Churchwardens, 74
Cider, 80, 81
Civil War, 15, 33, 46
Classical Foot, 20, 21
Clay Trade, 48, 70, **73**, 82
Clayton, John, 44
Clifton, 40
Cloth, see Textile Industry
Coaches and Coaching Inns, 50, **51**, 63-64; Stage coaches, 67
Coal, 44
Cobb (Lyme Regis), 9-11
Cockeril, Thomas, 34
Coker, Rev. John, 40
Colby, General, 68
Collins, Captain Greenvile, 58

Common Ground, **96**, 97-98
Common Land, 73
Common Rights, 28, 48
Commons, The (Shaftesbury), 66
Conder, Thomas, 60-62, **61**
Contour Lines, 52
Contraband, 55
Conventional Signs and Symbols, 11, 12, 17, 38, 39, 48, 52, **56**, 57, 72, 81, 85-86, 89, 93
Coppice, 87
Coppice Street (Shaftesbury), 67
Coral, 24
Cordite Factory, 97
Corfe Castle, 10, 15, 28, 34, 43, 60, 63, 70, 85, **88**
Corfe Mullen, 85
Corn, 24, 48, 73
Cornhill (London), 34, 78
Cornwall, 66
Corscombe, 57
Cosmography and Geography (Blome), 28
County Boundaries, Redrawing of, 8, 12-13, 90-91
County Councils, 12, 46, 64
County Reference Library, 97
Coupar House (Blandford), 71, **72**
Cowley, John, **43**, 43-44
Cox, Rev.Thomas, 34
Cranborne, 12, 33, 34, 37, 40, 46, 48, 55, 60, 64, 81
Cranborne Chase, 11, 40, 48
Cranborne Priory, 40, 48, 64
Creighton, R., 89
Crekelade, 11, 24, 28
Crewkerne, 30, 60, 78
Cromwell, Oliver, 33, 67
Cromwell, Thomas, 9
Crown Inn, Dorchester, 50, **51**
Culloden, Battle of, 68
Cumberland, Duke of, 68
Cunningham, 71
Customary Mile, 30; see also Miles
Cycling Maps, **93**, 96

Dairy-farming, 88
Dalton, William Hugh, 62
Dalwood, 90
Damer, John, 63
Danes, 32
'Danger Hills', 96
Dawes, Philip N., 86
Dawson, Lieutenant Robert K., R.E., 86
D-Day, 97
De la Lynde, Sir John, 20
De Mandeville, Baron Galfridus, 24
Deans Court (Wimborne), 88

Deans Leaze, 91
Deeping, Georges Bernard, 81
Deer and Deer Parks, 10, 11, **13**, 15, 20, 48, 78, 85
Dell, Clare, 98
Denham Film Studios, 97
Derby, 68
Devon, 12, 18, 32, 81, 91
Dewlish, 71
Dewlish House, 71, **72**, 85, 86
Dicey, Cluer, 15
Dictionary, Barclay's, 91, **92**
Dictionary of the English Language (Dr Johnson's), 63
Digby, Lord, 63, 91, **92**
Direction for the English Traviller, 24, **25**
Dissolution of the Monasteries, 40
Distance tables, 24-25, **25**, 34, 42, 43
Distances, 24-5, 30, 33, 34, 36, 42, 43, 46, 48, 63, 71, 76, 78, 81, 82, 83
Dockwra, William, 78
Dodington, Hon. George Bubb, 40, 63
Dodsley, James, 44; Robert, **43**, 44
Domesday Book, 15
Donne, Samuel, 57, 87
Dorchester, 18, 19, 24, 25, 33, 39, 43, 48, 63, 67, 71, 81, 85, 97; Arms of, 34, 60, **61**, 91, **92**, 97; Crown Inn, 50; Keep Military Museum, 97; Roman Amphitheatre, **39**; Roman Wall, 18; Town Plan, 18, **19**
Dorchester and Wool Turnpike Trust, 60;
Dorset, passim
Dorset and Somerset Canal, 76
Dorset buttons, 26-27, 44
Dorset Constabulary, 97
Dorset, Countess of, 21
Dorset County Council, 12
Dorset County M.P.s, 43; see also Parliament
Dorset County Record Office, 57, 87, 88
Dorset, Earls of, 18, **19**
Dorset, Marquis of, 8, **19**, 27
Dorset Rural Music School, 83
Dorset in Wartime, 97
Dorset Walks, Pathfinder Guide (Jarrold-OS), 93
Dorsetshire, Survey of, 40
Dover, 78, 81
Down House, 84
Downe Street (Bridport), 66
Downs (Kingston Lacy), 57
Downton, 83
Doyley, John, 57
Drax, Thomas Erle, 63

List of Subscribers

The publishers would like to thank all those whose names are listed below,
as well as the many subscribers who chose to remain anonymous.
Their support, and interest in the history of Dorset maps, helped make this book possible.

Edythe Mary Ackerman
Betty Florence Adkins (neé Farrow)
Rosemary Allen
H.K. Allsopp
Kathleen Andersen
Revd. J.F. Andrews
Ian K.D. Andrews, M.A. (Oxon)
Ray and Liz Arkell
Neil Arnold
Library, Ashdown School
David Ashford
J.R. Askew
Simon Austin
Mary B. Axford (neé Cook)
Keith Aylen
Martin Ayres

Alison Bailey
J.N. Baird
F.N.R. Ballam
Phyllis Gwendolen Ballam
E.W. Ballem
Dr. Peter Balson
Chris Barber
Robin Barbour
Mr. K. Barker
Dennis Barlow
Professor and Mrs. J.A. Barnard
Jack Barnes
John R. Bartlett
Libby Batchelor
David J. Batten
Alec and Eleanor Baxter
Mr. & Mrs. Roger Baynton-Williams
Alan Beadle
Mike Beams
Margaret Beaton

Martin Beaton
Michael Beaton
Richard J. Beaton
Ella Maisy Beaton-Rekkers
Jake Jeroen Beaton-Rekkers
Peter Bell
June Bennett
Wayne Bennett
Henry Best
Stephen Binnington
Mr. F.M.StL. Bircher
John Bishop
Adrian Bishop-Laggett
Cdr. John Bithell, O.B.E. Royal Navy
A.J. Blad
John and Frances Boarder
Robert Boas
Mr. Grant I. Bocking
Fanny Boltsa
Mike Bone
Mr. & Mrs. M. Bonham Cozens
Carole Bonifas
Mrs. Joan E. Booth
Ed Bowditch
Maureen Bowler
John V. Boys
Diana Bradley
Mrs. Richard Bridges
Patricia M. Brindley
Karen Brittin
Maggi Broadbent
Mike & Heather Brookman
S.J. Brown
Alan J. Brown
David Brown
John F. Brown
Montague A.J. & Sybil A. Brown

Peter J. Brown
Sandra Brown
Stuart Browning
James Bryant
Joseph Bucklin Society
Viv Budd
Adam Budden
Richard F. Burden
Richard Burleigh
Elizabeth Burton
Terry, Jenny & Mark Butler

M.J. Cahill
John Campbell-Kease
Ann Capon
Vanessa Carlyon
R.A. Carroll
Mr. & Mrs. M.A. Carter
Jack Cassell
Bryan Cassidy
Don and Fran Chalfont
Stephen B. Chapman
Chardstock Historical Record Group
Paul and Diana Cheater
Miss P. Chesney
John Childs
John Christmas
Christopher N. Churchill
Eddie Clark
H. Clark Dean
Peter C. Clarke
John & Anne Coates
Margaret Collier
Ray Collins
Frank Arthur Collinson, FCA
Sadie & Alan Coney
Kathleen Copeland

Penny Copland-Griffiths
J.K. Cordy
Mr. & Mrs. T.W.G. Corry
Matthew Cripps
Janice Croad
Robyn Crocker
Richard Crumbleholme
Colin Cuff
A.J. Cumming

Richard & Angela D'Silva
George & Ann Dannatt
Ian L. Davies
T.E. Davies
Charles E. Davis
Stephen Dawson
Victoria de Maré
Philip M. de Paris
Chris Deaves
Colonel C.J.G. Delamain
John Denniss
Kenneth F. Dibben
Kenneth Dibben
Jane Dibdin
Pam Dinsdale
Mrs Helen D. Doble
Mrs. Donell
Greg & Alison Dorey
Mike & Chris Dorey
Peter George Dorey
Dorset County Council, Rights of Way
Dorset Natural History &
    Archaeological Society
F.J. Douch
S. Dunford
Christopher Durant
Barbara Dye

James Edwards
Quentin Edwards
Keith Eldred
Susan Elkin
Jennie and Brian Ellis
Richard C. Elwell
Colin Elworthy
Primrose and Meyrick Emrys-Roberts
Mrs Susan Emsley
English Nature, Dorset Team
Paul C. Ensom
Michael and Ann Evans

Irene Fearnside (*neé* Bellenger)
John Ferris
Mrs. Brenda D. Flint
Mr. W.H.F. Foot
Ben M. Ford
Douglas K. Fox
Steve & Linda Frampton
Brian Freake
Michael J. French
Robin & Peggy Frith
A.E.H. and Mrs. G. Frost
C.R. Fry
Roy Fursey

John Gadd
M.O. Gale
Victor E. Gale
Brian J. Galpin
Mrs. S.B. Gane
Simon Gatrell
Peter Gibbons
Ian Gilbert
David Glassock
M.R. Goddard
Joan Goldsbrough
Robin Goldsbrough
Jean Goodall
Ivan Gould
June Grant
Gordon J. Green
Jillian Ann Green
Harry Grenville
Harry Grenville
Eileen Grierson
James T. Grinter
James Grocott
L.B.R. Groves
Mary Groves

Adrian Hadley
A.W. Hall
David L. Hall
Ray and Irene Hall
Dr. Richard Hall
Sir Michael Hanham, Bt
Edward John Hann
Gavin & Ann Hannah
Michael A. Hansford
Philip John Hansford
John Harding
Mrs. Stella F. Hardy
Mr. & Mrs. P.D.G. Hares
Vera Harrington
Professor Duncan Harris
Robin & Elizabeth Harris
K.K. Hart
Frank Harwood
Dr. Peter Hatherley
Andrew Hawkes
Mrs. S. Hawkins
Murray Hawkins Dental Practice
John Francis Haysom
Geoffrey Hayward
Nina Hayward
Mrs. Julie Hazlett
Mary Head
Diane Heard
Trevor Hearl
R.N. Heaton
Dr. J.M. Hedges
Brian Heeley
Mark Helfer
Nancy, Lady Henley
I. Hewitt
John Hill
Narelle Hill
Shelagh M. Hill
John A. Hilton King
David J.B. Hindley
John Hinton
Gerald T. Hoare
David J. Hoddinott
Brian Holden
Brian Hollins
C.J.C. Hooper
Ralph Hopton
David Vincent Horlock
Dr. Simon Horner
Mrs. Horsey and Mr. Bridle
Anne Horsfall
Anne Hosford

Christopher Hounsell
David Sanctuary Howard
Mrs. F.M. Howard-Glydon
Geoffrey D. Hucklebridge
Ben & James Hughes
Dr. & Mrs. Bryn C. Hughes
Miss Philidda C. Hughes
David Hulmes
Brena Humm
The Huntington Library

Brenda Innes

The Revd. Edward & Mrs. Sara
   Jacson
Elisabeth James
Jude James
Mr. & Mrs. Brian James
Peter and Bridgit James
Robert Jenvey
Joan Johnson
Gillian Ann Johnson (*neé* Thomas)
Helen S. Jones
Joan & John Jones
Oliver D. ap Alun Jones
Richard P.A. Jones
Stella Jones

Jane Kellock
David Kendall
Prof. and Mrs. C.R. Kennedy
Ruby Kinch
Angela King
Anne & Michael King
John B. Kirkbride
Gavin Kirkpatrick
Mr. & Mrs. Paul Knocker

Malcolm Lacey
Winifred Ettie Land
Mr. R.F. Lane
W.J. Langdon
Ted & Denise Lanning
Dr. and Mrs. J.A. Larkin
John Nicholas Lauderdale
Dr. Ian Lawrence
Phil Lawrence
Miss Sue Lawrence
Robert Holden Lazenby
Michael and Pam le Bas
Richard & Tamsin Lee
E.M.J. Leleu

Michael Lester
John Lewis
Moyra Lindsay
Hugh Lindsay
Anne Lloyd
Tim and Bridget Loasby
Prof. C.J.S. Lock
Henry Lock
Dr. Peter Lock
Richard Lock
Frank and Giles Lockyer
Mrs P.M. Lockyer
G.J. Lodder
Roger Lord
Keith Lovelock
David and Vivian Lowe
Stephen Luck
Dr. David Lush
Elizabeth Lyon

Charles A. Maber
Mr. & Mrs. A.H. Maccoy
Michael Macey
Mrs. Barbara Marriott
Roland F. Marsden
Alan W. Marsh
Brian Martin
C.J.B. & M.M. Martin
Chris Martin
Mr. and Mrs. C.R.B. Martin
Mrs. J.E. Maule
Mr. & Mrs. A.T. May
Mr. D.E. Maybury
Alastair & Rosemary McDonald
Sally McLaren
Joan McNabb
Caroline Meatyard
Elizabeth Joy Meech
John A. Meer
John Menlove
R.M. Mercer
Alan J. Miller
Ian R. Norie Miller
Michael Millgate
Derek Mills
Marian Mills
Peter W.T. Mills
Dr. R.W. Mills
J.K. Milner
Christopher Moore
Colin Moore
Sandie Moors

Audrey Moreton
Mrs. Iris A. Morris
Margaret Mortimer
Alan Morton
Roland S. Moss
Mr. & Mrs. Patrick Moule
Lynda Mudle-Small
Tim Mullen
Elinor Murphy
D. Myerscough
Frank Myerscough

Joan Nash
Rockley Nash
L.R. & W.G. Nayler
P.A. Neale
N.R. Newbery
John A. Newbould
John Newton
Patricia Newton
Christopher Nicholson
A.W. & M.E. Nineham
Andrew Nineham
Peter C.G. Nolan
Mrs. Ann Norbury
Janet Norgate
Dr. Peter Northover

Richard Ollard
Neville L. Orchard, M.A.
Nicholas R. Orman
A.O. Ormerod
David Orr
Colonel M.A.C. Osborn
Dennis J. Ould
D. Overy
Pauline Owen
John Oxford

Krid Panyarachun
L.J.H. Parke
Dr. J. Parker
Peter Parnwell
Christopher Parsons
I.D. Pascall
John W. Patrick
Mr. & Mrs. J.G.C. Patterson
Bernard and Christine Paull
Mr. R.N.R. Peers
John Peirce
Mr. & Mrs. J.T. Perkins
Colin R. Perris

Charles Pettit
John and Barbara Phillips
S.H. Pickett
F.P. Pitfield
Mr. & Mrs. V.J. Platt
Ernest Plowman
Mrs. Laurence Pollard
Carol Pomeroy
Tony Pomeroy
Valerie Pontin
Joan Poock
Nicola Powell
Dr. R.P. & Mrs. H.J. Power
Jeremy D. Powne
E. Lewis Poyle
Mrs C.M. Puckett

David Rabone
F. Radcliffe
Judy Ramsey
Paul Randall
Victor Ransome
P.S. Read
Mr. Stephen Reade
Bill & Mavis Reed
Gordon A. Reed
Ken T.W. Rees
Margaret Rehahn
Robert Rennie
Nigel Reynolds
Paul & Shuzhen Richards
Barry M. Rideout
Richard Riding
David E. Ridout
John P. Riley
Phil and Marion Roberts
Eric Roberts
V.J. Roberts
Lucy Robins
Olive and Ivor Robinson
Parry and Juliet Rogers
Elizabeth Russell-Gaunt
Jo & Jan Rutter

John M. Sanders
Peter Saunders
R.J. Saville
Mrs. J.E. Scully
Mrs. Janet K.L. Seal
Gordon W.H. Sealy
Marilyn W. Sealy
Shirley & Bryan Sefton-Smith

Shaftesbury Historical Society
Elizabeth Sharp
Edwin Shearing
Larissa Sheehan
Ann Sheridan
Margaret Shipton
Edwina Jane Shooter
John Simmons
Paul Simpson
Poppy Simpson
Andrew Skipsey
John Slatford
John Slattery
Dennis Smale
Dr. Isobel A. Smart
Alex H.J. Smith
Andrew Graham Smith
D.F. Smith
Doreen Smith
J.R. Smith
K.G.S. Smith
Lynette and Frank Smith
Mr. M.C. Smith
R.W. Snaydon
Dr. C.A. Snodgrass
Maureen Southerden
Ronald Staniforth
Susan V. Stanley
Ian Staple
Rupert Stebbings
Derek F. Stevens
John Stickland
Mary Stobbs
Mrs. Bennie Streeter
Adrian Stuart
Leofric Studd
Diana Summers
Terry Sweeney

Dr. Henry Teed
Geoffrey Teychenne
Lloyd N. Thomas
Raymond A. Thomas
Michael A. Tombs
Paul N. Tomlinson
Rev. Dr. John Travell
Mr. R.R. Travers
Katherine Treanor
D.J.Y. Trehane
William Trevelyan Thomas
K. Joyce Trott
L. Joyce Trott

Brenda Tunks
Margaret B. Turner

Jackie Upton

David & Linda Viner

David and Leonora Walker
Mrs. A.M.J. Walker
Dr. P.E. Wallis
Jan & Geoffrey Wansell
Miss Beryl J. Ward
Warden family
Delia Wareham
Elizabeth Warren
A.B. Warrick
Hazel & Jim Waterworth
Marion Watson
Mr. Leonard A. Way
His Honour Judge David Maclaren
    Webster Q.C.
John & Maureen Weeks
Caroline Wells
Pamela Wenden
Shirley M. West
Lesley Weston
K.V. Wheller
David John White
David P. White
Shelagh Whitehouse
D.S. Whitelegge
K.P. Wightman
Malcolm Wilcox
Richard Wilding
Jeremy Wilkes
Anne-Marie Wilkinson
Ian Willis
Rupert Willoughby
John F. Willsher
Mr. & Mrs. K. Wingfield Digby
R.L.C. Wood
Anne Wood
Nick Woods
Dr. Ann Woodward
Robert Woolner
Kenneth P. Wortley
Michael R. Wright
Nigel & Sue Wyatt

Mrs Elisabeth Young
Mrs. Mary Yoward